The New York Times

FAVORITE DAY CROSSWORDS: MONDAY
75 of Your Favorite Very Easy Monday Crosswords from
The New York Times

Edited by Will Shortz

ST. MARTIN'S GRIFFIN ⚏ NEW YORK

The New York Times

FAVORITE DAY CROSSWORDS: MONDAY

ACROSS

1 Word before "of health" or "of directors"
6 Adroit
10 Notion
14 See eye to eye
15 Lamb's nom de plume
16 Netting
17 Makes a good start
20 Understand
21 Mr. Onassis
22 Celebrity
23 Bearing
24 Common Market money
25 Isolated
32 Peter and Paul, e.g., but not Mary
33 Defeat decisively
34 Eggs
36 It marches on
37 Bar seat
39 Nasty, as a comment
40 ___ of a kind
41 Caesar and Vicious, e.g.
42 Radarange maker
43 Attempt to win approval
47 Enemy
48 Lasses' mates
49 Blueprint
53 Letter before omega
54 Jiang Qing's husband
57 Trying hard
60 Sicilian spouter
61 Intend
62 Architectural style
63 Light for serenaders
64 Terrier type
65 Parisian river

DOWN

1 Catches, as game
2 S-shaped curve
3 Jovial Johnson
4 Legal matter
5 Holds in custody
6 Emulate Webster
7 Inventor Whitney
8 Evergreens
9 Not gross
10 Stain
11 Conked out, as a battery
12 Conoco competitor
13 "Pardon me . . ."
18 Oka River city
19 Unspoken
23 Bog
25 "Beetle Bailey" pooch
26 Taking advantage of
27 Not as wild
28 "The Road Not Taken" poet
29 Besides
30 Like the 11:00 news, usually
31 Gulf of Riga tributary
35 Call it ___ (stop working)
37 Pistols, swords, etc.
38 N.F.L. scores
39 Sound equipment
41 Sleep loudly
42 More than devotees
44 Kabul native
45 Type of skiing
46 Boss Tweed nemesis
49 Carpe ___
50 Division word
51 ___ time (never)
52 Earth inheritors, with "the"
54 The south of France
55 Forthwith
56 Folklore villain
58 Remunerate
59 Cry's partner

by Kenneth Witte

2

ACROSS

1 Tijuana's locale, informally
5 Pro ___ (proportionately)
9 Amount bet
14 Pagan god
15 Decorative pitcher
16 Electrical pioneer Nikola
17 Valley
18 Witch's blemish
19 "All hope abandon, ye who ___ here!"
20 Home addition
21 Century-old time
23 Polk's successor
25 Auction
26 McGuffey book
29 Kind of measles
33 Scrooge's visitor
35 Circus employee
37 Sooner than
38 Furor
39 Bates, for one
40 Barbra's "A Star is Born" co-star
41 Secret ending
42 Jockey rival
43 Buenos ___
44 Fright
46 Exquisite
48 Ancient land east of the Tigris
50 Prepared, as tomatoes
53 Roy Rogers's theme song
58 "Sweet as apple cider" girl
59 TV soldiers of fortune
60 N.F.L. coach Jim
61 Tennis score
62 Newswoman Shriver
63 ___ even keel
64 Investor's purchase
65 Rear
66 Darn
67 Influence

DOWN

1 Bathroom fixture
2 ___ Rogers St. Johns
3 Blackbeard few one
4 Totality
5 Finder's fee
6 "Begone!"
7 Sea swallow
8 Cager Gilmore
9 Three Rivers Stadium player
10 Campground denizen
11 ___ spumante
12 Swiss painter
13 Roasting items
21 One with kids
22 Conrad of "The Kiss"
24 ___ majesté
27 Thames town
28 Appraised
30 Lehár operetta, with "The"
31 Indy 500's Luyendyk
32 Eliot of "The Untouchables"
33 It's stuck in beach sandals
34 Contain
36 Miniplateau
39 Corday's victim
40 Pass, as a forged check
42 Francis of Assisi, e.g.
43 Aardvark's meal
45 Fix
47 Hispaniola, e.g.
49 1983 Michael Keaton film
51 Minneapolis suburb
52 Beaut
53 Easter dinners
54 Rat ___
55 Balzac's "Le ___ Goriot"
56 Tiptop
57 Kurdish home
61 Stomach muscles, for short

by Gregory E. Paul

ACROSS

1 Canyon sound
5 Cross-legged exercises
9 August forecast
14 Bumbler
15 50–50
16 Mohawk Valley city
17 Kitchen fat
18 Shea Stadium nine
19 Pressed one's luck
20 Big-eared animal
21 Vacation locale
23 In ___ (ready for release)
25 Sign of summer
26 Cordage
29 It's printed in the back
34 Gerald Ford's birthplace
36 Banned apple spray
38 By way of
39 Vacation locale
42 Declare
43 Congressman Gingrich
44 Solemn procedures
45 "___ forget"
47 1959 Fiestas song
49 Comic Charlotte
51 Outcome
54 Vacation locale
60 Have a tab
61 Like gold
62 On-the-cob treat
63 Ilsa of "Casablanca"
64 Wrist movement
65 Tale starter
66 Pre-owned
67 Army vehicles (You're welcome!)

68 Blue-green
69 Jolly, to the British

DOWN

1 Brilliance
2 Sharply disagree
3 Monmouth Park events
4 ___ man out
5 Sana native
6 "Back to you"
7 Fetches
8 Photographer Adams
9 Rock of Hollywood
10 Jazz locale
11 Muralist Joan
12 Cake decorator
13 Janet Reno's home county
21 Lacquer

22 Pine
24 Associate
27 Put the finger on
28 Is brilliant
30 Painter's mishaps
31 Russian parliament building
32 Sea swooper
33 "Broom Hilda" creator Myers
34 Whitish gem
35 Military command?
37 "Wheels"
40 Late-late show hour
41 Vacation events
46 Violent downfalls
48 Tornado part
50 Orlando attraction
52 Shareholder

53 Sleepwear item
54 ___-Hartley Act
55 Hip-shaking in Kauai
56 Actress Moran
57 Rube
58 TV knob
59 Whale of a movie
63 Broadway hit of 1964–65

by Thomas W. Schier

4

ACROSS

1 "Shane" star
5 Late actor Phoenix
10 "Dark Lady" singer, 1974
14 "__ in a manger . . ."
15 Author Zola
16 "___, from New York . . ."
17 Haircuts?
19 Kathleen Battle offering
20 "__ we having fun yet?"
21 Glowing
22 Kuwaiti structure
24 Opening word
26 Broadway show based on a comic strip
27 Dubuque native
29 Imperturbable
33 Become frayed
36 Former spouses
38 Conceited smile
39 Hawkeye portrayer
40 Recording auditions
42 Garfield's canine pal
43 Pilots let them down
45 Cushy
46 Catches some Z's
47 It fugits
49 Gullible
51 Sufficient
53 Knucklehead
57 Horoscope heading
60 Police blotter abbr.
61 Prospector's find
62 World rotator?
63 Fake embroidery?
66 Augury
67 "This way in" sign
68 __ carotene
69 Emcee Parks
70 Nursery packets
71 Flowery verses

DOWN

1 Actor Lorenzo
2 Conscious
3 Odense residents
4 Recolor
5 Critiqued
6 ". . . __ a man with seven wives"
7 __ ordinaire
8 "Candle in the Wind" singer __ John
9 Copal and others
10 Vandalized art work?
11 Put on staff
12 Heinous
13 Kind of estate
18 Movie Tarzan __ Lincoln
23 Whoppers
25 Smog?
26 Showy flower
28 Lumber camp implements
30 Verdi heroine
31 Stumble
32 Makes do, with "out"
33 Float
34 Madame's pronoun
35 Eden resident
37 Divan
41 Scoundrels
44 Its usefulness goes to waste
48 Cumin and cardamom
50 Test tube
52 Actor Greene
54 Courted
55 Livid
56 Ann Richards's bailiwick
57 Poor fellow
58 "Be our guest!"
59 Concluded
60 Thunderstruck
64 Part of a year in Provence
65 Cable add-on

by Norma Steinberg

ACROSS

1 Atop
5 Clubbed
10 Motes
14 New York Cosmos star
15 Chou ___
16 Oklahoma tribesman
17 Lord Nelson site
20 Part of an electrical switch
21 Zeroes
22 Hectored
23 Sans verve
24 Medicament
27 Winter woe
28 Ottoman official
31 The Donald's ex
32 Fly like Lindbergh
33 Aits in Arles
34 Prepare for an Indian attack
37 Raison d'___
38 30's actress Grey and others
39 Nighttime noise
40 Beam
41 Sponsorship
42 Feeds a furnace
43 Belgian river
44 Baseball union boss Donald
45 Like llamas
48 Sends quickly
52 Ships' drop-off location?
54 Sea flyer
55 Gnawed away
56 Composition closure
57 Crazy bird?
58 Monopoly payments
59 Formerly

DOWN

1 Goes (for)
2 ___ Beach, Fla.
3 Airline to Jerusalem
4 Testimonial
5 It's hummed
6 1973 hit by the Rolling Stones
7 Covered
8 The "E" in E.N.T
9 Prohibit
10 Wampum
11 I-70's western terminus
12 Ilk
13 Golf course 18
18 Of some electrodes
19 Printer's spacer
23 Tree trunks
24 Potato preparer
25 "Requiem for ___" (Broadway song)
26 Take the plunge
27 Lawyer Roy M. and others
28 "Take ___ at this!"
29 Type
30 Bridge of ___ (Euclid proposition)
32 Way up?
33 Blissful state?
35 Produce
36 Wheezing cause
41 Birthright seller
42 TV listing
43 Modern-day Sheba
44 Tops
45 Ex-steelworkers chief
46 Fiery fiddler
47 1962 Bond villain
48 Solar disk
49 Mr. Stravinsky
50 Lawyers' degrees
51 Install in office
53 "___ you sure?"

by Joel Davajan

6

ACROSS

1 Gore's "___ in the Balance"
6 One who's "agin" it
10 Train unit
13 "___ Without Windows" ('64 song)
14 Supermarket meat label
15 Territory
16 Major Bowes updated?
18 Fat
19 Home on the range
20 Kind of signal
21 Part of SEATO
22 Mail HQ
23 Breakfast order
25 Lift up
29 Woodworker's choice
32 Belgian airline
34 Bests
38 Hemingway opus
41 Dub again
42 Took ten
43 Ingenious
45 Shows remorse
46 Up
50 Marinaro and others
52 Slough
53 Reckon
56 Bosom companions
60 "Remember the neediest," e.g.
61 Olympia Dukakis film
63 Fast time
64 Capri, for one
65 Misrepresent
66 Pupil's place
67 African lake
68 Volvo worker

DOWN

1 Bridge seat
2 Comic Johnson
3 Imitation morocco
4 Civil wrong
5 ___ Pinafore
6 Cottonwoods
7 Grammy-winning pianist
8 Yacht heading
9 Person of will
10 1929 event
11 High nest
12 "M*A*S*H" character
15 "Too bad!"
17 Paraspsychology study
22 Authentic
24 Singing sisters
25 D.C. zone
26 Comic Bert
27 Have ___ in one's bonnet
28 Probe
30 Flat sign?
31 Vienna is its cap.
33 In opposition to one another
35 River to the Seine
36 Town near Padua
37 Osmose
39 Melmackian of TV
40 60's org.
44 Craved
46 With room to spare
47 "Little Orphant Annie" poet
48 Goodnight girl
49 Pants part
51 ___ Plaines
54 Deluxe
55 Southeast Kansas town
56 Witch's ___
57 Golden, e.g.
58 Tart
59 ___ Ball (arcade game)
62 Kitchen meas.

by Sidney L. Robbins

ACROSS

- **1** Like Job
- **8** Bob or beehive
- **14** Leisurely musical pieces
- **15** Decrees
- **17** Pentagon advocate?
- **19** Parlor piece
- **20** Ex-Knick coach Jackson
- **21** Author of "Life in London"
- **22** Heart of France
- **24** Part
- **25** Visit Robert Reich?
- **31** Medical apprentice
- **32** Ease
- **37** Blue "Yellow Submarine" characters
- **38** Revised
- **40** Ancient beginning
- **41** Off course
- **42** Foggy Bottom boat?
- **46** Narc's collar
- **50** "Since ___ Have You"
- **51** Not for
- **52** Juan's uncle
- **53** Pescadores neighbor
- **59** Reno's piano practice?
- **62** Tympanic membrane
- **63** Guides, in a way
- **64** Brews tea
- **65** Menu listings

DOWN

- **1** Falsifies accounts
- **2** Chick ender
- **3** White House heavyweight
- **4** Beach Boys' "___ Around"
- **5** "___ kleine Nachtmusik"
- **6** Titan tip
- **7** Poetic monogram
- **8** Spa installation
- **9** Maestro Toscanini
- **10** Words often exchanged
- **11** Twice as unlikely
- **12** Down Under dog
- **13** "Love Story" star
- **16** January 1 song ending
- **18** Riding the waves
- **23** Bullfight cries
- **25** Walk with difficulty
- **26** Unwanted classification, once
- **27** Printing style: Abbr.
- **28** Hawaiian state bird
- **29** Kingston and others
- **30** Fee schedule
- **33** Friend of Ernie
- **34** Sills solo
- **35** Caterpillar construction
- **36** Advantage
- **38** Calling company
- **39** Intersection maneuver
- **43** Asks for a loan
- **44** They trip up foreigners
- **45** Magician's sound effect
- **46** First or home, e.g.
- **47** Last of the Mohicans
- **48** Genesis
- **49** Spanish squiggle
- **54** ___ were (so to speak)
- **55** Ovid's way
- **56** Oenologist's interest
- **57** Entr'___
- **58** Costner character
- **60** Prior, to Prior
- **61** G.I. ___

by Randolph Ross

8

ACROSS

1 Hearth debris
6 Atmosphere
10 Columnist Bombeck
14 Room to ___
15 Skater Heiden
16 High time?
17 Critical juncture
20 Parade
21 Some oranges
22 Roasting items
25 Sometimes they get the hang of it
26 Woolly one
30 Carnegie Hall event
32 Where Marco Polo traveled
33 Tomb tenant
34 All fired up?
37 Future brass
41 Modeled, maybe
42 Mountain ridge
43 Peruvian of yore
44 Neptune's fork
46 Physicist Niels
47 Work, work, work
49 Its password was "Mickey Mouse"
51 Trotsky rival
52 Straight shooters?
57 Stops rambling
61 Algerian seaport
62 Broadway groom of 1922
63 Sister of Thalia
64 Bridge seat
65 Bank holding
66 Prepare to shave

DOWN

1 Cleo's snakes
2 Flyspeck
3 "Let the Sunshine in" musical
4 Sea bird
5 Bristles
6 W.W. I grp.
7 Mausoleum item
8 "Road to ___"
9 Beginnings of poetry?
10 Involve
11 Beauty aid
12 Folkways
13 Writer Beattie and others
18 Poet translated by FitzGerald
19 Toledo locale
23 Depended
24 Perfumed
26 Senate output

27 On the briny
28 "Gorillas in the ___"
29 Hit a fly, perhaps
31 Mean
34 Host Jay
35 Yen
36 Ivan, for one
38 Church front area
39 Expensive rug
40 Fish in a way
44 Aptitude
45 Weight allowance
47 Pack away
48 "Falcon Crest" star
50 "Egad!"
51 Barge
53 McHenry, e.g.
54 Münchhausen, for one

55 Within: Prefix
56 Common sign
58 Sash
59 Cause for overtime
60 Clucker

by Sidney L. Robbins

ACROSS

1 Child's getaway
5 Nurse's stick
9 Malpractice target
14 Margarine
15 Part of a cash register
16 Sam or Tom, e.g.
17 Businessperson's oxymoron
20 Crowbar
21 Runner Devers
22 Sums
23 "Get __!"
25 Cut up
27 Vipers
30 Indignant person's oxymoron
35 Actor Erwin
36 Breezy
37 Refer (to)
38 Dinner bird
40 Command to Fido
42 Jewish dinner
43 Mideast language
45 Flood survivor
47 W.W. II grp.
48 Oxymoron for a homely person
50 Cheek
51 Riches' opposite
52 Took a powder
54 Jacob's brother
57 Bare
59 Speechify
63 Coffee drinker's oxymoron
66 Passé
67 Within: Prefix
68 Model married to David Bowie
69 Steeple
70 Slumber
71 Library item

DOWN

1 Monk's hood
2 Lotion ingredient
3 Former talk-show host
4 Fireplace equipment
5 Penn, e.g.: Abbr.
6 Belly dancers
7 Edison's middle name
8 Mathematician Pascal
9 Sine __ non
10 Straighten out
11 Sarcasm
12 Dolt
13 Barbies' mates
18 Enrage
19 Bow of silents
24 Black bird
26 Three-time Super Bowl-winning coach
27 Tin Pan Alley org.
28 One of the Beatles
29 Chrysalises
31 In competition
32 Lindley of "The Ropers"
33 Creativity
34 Indoor balls
36 Writer Loos
39 Busybody
41 Stashes
44 Caesar's swans
46 Certain vote
49 Shylock
50 Magellan, e.g.
53 Lee to Grant
54 Concludes
55 It's seen in bars
56 Against
58 Unit of force
60 BB's
61 Word after "go!"
62 Sea eagle
64 Humorist George
65 "Oh, darn!"

by Janie Lyons

10

ACROSS
1 Wrongs
5 Stockyard group
9 Sail supports
14 Govt. agents
15 War of 1812 battle site
16 Member of a crowd scene
17 Give stars to
18 Basketball's Chamberlain
19 1993 Formula One winner Prost
20 Old "House Party" host
23 Knocks down
24 Reserved
25 1975 Stephanie Mills musical, with "The"
28 Hot time in Paris
29 Take turns
33 Kind of package
34 More albinolike
35 Phobic
37 P.G.A.'s 1992 leading money winner
39 Rickey Henderson stat
41 Hunter of myth
42 Well ventilated
43 Least exciting
45 Rotary disk
48 Sign of summer
49 Mathematician's letters
50 Throw
52 N.F.L. receiver for 18 seasons
57 Booby
59 Not in use
60 Crips or Bloods
61 Uris's "__ Pass"
62 Baylor mascot
63 Skirt
64 Check writer

65 Slumped
66 Actress Charlotte et al.

DOWN
1 Attack by plane
2 Turkish hostelry
3 Stinging plant
4 Fish-line attachment
5 Axed
6 Dancer Bruhn
7 Small brook
8 Loathe
9 Substantial
10 Wheel shaft
11 Noted film trilogy
12 Angle starter
13 __ Jose
21 Hebrew for "contender with God"

22 Eponymous poet of Greek drama
26 Temper
27 British alphabet ender
30 Elderly one
31 Gumshoe
32 "__ With a View"
33 Columnist Herb
34 Supplicate
36 Thread of life spinner, in myth
37 Savageness
38 Late actress Mary
39 NaCl, to a pharmacist
40 Truss
44 Deviates from the script
45 Party to Nafta

46 Exact retribution
47 Enters a freeway
49 Persian Gulf land
51 Trevanian's "The __ Sanction"
53 Green target
54 Madison Avenue product
55 Ardor
56 Boor
57 Cutup
58 Noche's opposite

by Janet R. Bender

ACROSS

1 Wealthy person
5 Takes advantage of
9 "The Forsyte ___"
13 Likeness
15 Kind of stick
16 Sheriff Tupper of "Murder, She Wrote"
17 Social hangout
19 Sea swallow
20 Home turnover
21 Knock out of kilter
23 Illuminated
24 Terminator
25 Bear up there
29 Steep slope
33 Crier of Greek myth
35 Wakens
39 Bettor's challenge
43 Show fright
44 Weird
45 Followed orders
48 N.Y. Police ___
49 Exodus priest
53 Mauna ___
55 Responded unintelligibly
58 "Last stop! ___!"
62 Abner's pal and namesakes
63 Diamond coup
66 Relative of the flute
67 Auction actions
68 Indian boat
69 Part of Halloween makeup
70 Church nook
71 Endure

DOWN

1 Informal greetings
2 Eastern V.I.P.
3 Wind instrument?
4 They'll be hunted in April
5 Big sports news
6 Loudly weep
7 "Holy moly!"
8 Kind of loser
9 Beelzebub
10 Change
11 Watkins Glen, e.g.
12 "Lou Grant" star
14 Lod airport airline
18 Nobelist Wiesel
22 Esteem
25 German link
26 Kind of squad
27 Lemonlike
28 Singer Lane
30 Cuomo's predecessor
31 Son of Prince Valiant
32 Australian hopper
34 Long Island town
36 Tool storage area
37 Limerick site
38 Barber's cut
40 Wane
41 Bullring shout
42 Receive
46 Pass
47 Cabbage Patch item
49 Visibly happy
50 Caribbean getaway
51 "___ has it . . ."
52 Start
54 Actor Guinness
56 Old lab burner
57 Trapdoor
59 Milky gem
60 Arm bone
61 Pueblo town
64 Employee card and others
65 Still and all

by Sidney L. Robbins

ACROSS

1 More exuberant, as a laugh
5 Snatch
9 "Cold hands, ___"
14 Mast-steadying rope
15 Hitchcock's "___ Window"
16 Of a region
17 Now's partner
18 Eggshell
19 Rubberneck
20 Altar in the sky
21 Sault ___ Marie
22 Yarmulke
24 Capts.' subordinates
25 Campaign donor grp.
26 Some bikes
28 "___ the season . . ."
29 Upper regions of space
31 Scrabble piece
32 Mare's offspring
33 Judged
35 Place for E.M.K.
36 Concordes land there
37 Without reservation
40 Little demon
43 Corn site
44 Prolonged attacks
48 Steak order
49 Vesuvius's Sicilian counterpart
51 Boston Garden, e.g.
52 Gametes
53 Theater aide
55 White House defense grp.
56 Barbie's beau
57 Sixth sense
58 Joad and Kettle
59 Wilder's "___ Town"
60 Singer John
62 Gibbons
64 Desiccated
65 Means of connection
66 Gambler's "bones"
67 Like some cars
68 Pulse indication
69 Collectors' goals
70 February 14 symbol

DOWN

1 Like some candy boxes
2 Repeat
3 Otalgia
4 Place for ham and Swiss
5 Miss Garbo
6 Modern
7 Swiss river
8 Movie star with a kick?
9 Ethnic group portrayed in A. R. Gurney's plays
10 ___ Deco
11 Person who can move buildings
12 Kind of arts or law
13 With cruelty
21 ___ throat
23 Alters
27 Discourages
30 Overact
32 Where to go between acts
34 Restrains
38 Reporters' needs
39 Tale tellers
40 Jilted lover's woe
41 Entangler
42 Sanchez Vicario of tennis
45 Columbus, by birth
46 Guaranteed
47 University in Fairfield, Conn.
50 Mien
53 Slow on the uptake
54 Mitigates
61 Bouncer's demand
63 Pizza
64 California's Big ___

by Nancy Joline

13

ACROSS

1 Buddy
5 Balance sheet listing
10 Helper: Abbr.
14 New Rochelle college
15 They fly in formation
16 Wife of ___ (Chaucer pilgrim)
17 Ordnance
18 Fill with glee
19 Out of the weather
20 Battle in which Lee defeated Pope
23 Sunday talk: Abbr.
24 Activity
25 Fountain treat, for short
26 Battle in which Bragg defeated Rosecrans
31 Singer Coolidge et al.
32 Corner
33 11th-century date
36 Heaven on earth
37 Change
39 Earth sci.
40 Marry
41 Fine poker holdings
42 Hawks
43 Battle in which Grant defeated Bragg
46 John Wilkes Booth, e.g.
50 Tempe sch.
51 Items on a "must" list
52 Battle in which Lee defeated Burnside
57 Retread, e.g.
58 Go along (with)
59 Wrangler's pal
61 Overlook
62 Some are heroic
63 Mideast land
64 Promontory
65 Kilmer opus
66 Niño's nothing

DOWN

1 Spy grp.
2 Baseball, informally
3 Not deserved
4 Not fem.
5 Work to do
6 Infrequently
7 Petticoat junction
8 "Cómo ___ usted?"
9 Chelsea Clinton, e.g.
10 Embarrass
11 Nacho topping
12 Rib-eye
13 One's nearby
21 Dumbarton ___ (1944 meeting site)
22 P.D.Q.
23 Item in a hardware bin
27 Fire
28 Nuclear experiment
29 Coffee server
30 Start for fly or about
33 Three-hanky film
34 City once named for Stalin
35 Rick's beloved et al.
37 Herr's "Oh!"
38 "Cry ___ River"
39 General Motors make
41 Parcel of land
42 High-hat
44 Words before "I'm yours"
45 Tax
46 "Sweet" river of song
47 Record blot
48 Actress Garr et al.
49 Playwright Clifford
53 Engrossed
54 Mr. Stravinsky
55 Saskatchewan tribe
56 Atop
60 Kind of testing

by Jonathan Schmalzbach

14

ACROSS

1 Tot's talk, perhaps
5 Encourages
9 First-grade instruction
13 Stinks
15 "Thanks ___!"
16 Swing around
17 Like factory workers
19 U, for one
20 Elsie's bull
21 "Mommie ___" (Christina Crawford book)
23 "What's ___ for me?"
25 Take a potshot
26 Teller of white lies
29 Stage whisper
30 Give the eye
31 Quick bites
33 Advances
36 Baseball's Gehrig
37 Trunk
39 Runner Sebastian
40 Remains
43 Person of action
44 King's address
45 Illegal inducement
47 Mexican dishes
49 Speak-easy offering
50 Saxophonist Getz
51 Candid
53 Waiter's jotting
56 Actress Archer
57 Kind of jury
61 Bucks and does
62 Otherwise
63 Singer ___ Neville
64 Lawyer: Abbr.
65 Tackle-box item
66 City inside the Servian Wall

DOWN

1 Tennis shot
2 Run in neutral
3 Body's partner
4 Logician's start
5 Sidekick
6 Sum total
7 Wart giver, in old wives' tales
8 Emphasis
9 On a horse
10 Edit
11 No blessing, this!
12 Shipped
14 Fragrance
18 Marco Polo area
22 Dye color appropriate to this puzzle
24 Vacuum tube
26 Go belly up
27 Borodin's prince
28 Texas' state flower
29 Balance-sheet pluses
32 Golf club V.I.P.
34 Illustrator Gustave
35 Comprehends
38 Patrick Henry, e.g.
41 Bodega
42 Clothing specification
44 Boating hazard
46 Saharan tribesman
48 Newswoman Shriver
49 Intelligence-testing name
51 Actress Thompson
52 Glamour rival
54 River of Spain
55 Leeway
58 "It's no ___!"
59 Slippery one
60 Opposite SSW

by Sidney L. Robbins

ACROSS
1 Dumbfounded
5 Acquire, as expenses
10 Singer Campbell
14 Colombian city
15 Hughes's plane Spruce ___
16 1890's Vice President ___ P. Morton
17 1959 Rodgers and Hammerstein hit
20 "You can ___ horse to . . ."
21 Bridal path
22 Predicament
24 Obote's successor
26 1956 Comden-Green-Styne collaboration
33 On ___ (counting calories)
34 Man with a title
35 Soviet space vehicle
36 Pride and envy, e.g.
37 Old hat
38 "Aurora" painter
39 Kind of cap or cream
40 Radio host of note
41 First U.S.-born saint
42 1930 Gershwin musical
46 Sigmatism
47 Achy
48 Whiz kid
51 Blotto
54 1983 Herman-Fierstein musical
60 "Metamorphoses" poet
61 Wish granters
62 TV's Oscar
63 Hitches
64 Mill material
65 Murder

DOWN
1 Part of a play
2 Star of TV's "Wiseguy"
3 "Waiting for the Robert ___"
4 Puts out of commission
5 Desert critter
6 Persona ___ grata
7 How some packages are sent
8 R. & R. org.
9 Ring leader?
10 Sticking together
11 Decreasingly
12 Demonic
13 Garibaldi's birthplace
18 Keats or Shelley
19 Popular street name
23 Invent
24 Snaps handcuffs on
25 Gentle, as breezes
26 Grounds
27 Kingly decree
28 Passenger ship
29 Gobble
30 "___ man with seven . . ."
31 Curtain material
32 Nine-to-five routine
37 Conks out
38 Mutinied
41 ___-comic (play type)
43 Long narratives
44 Alan, Larry or Stephen
45 Tap-dance
48 Crushing news
49 Four-star review
50 ___ rain
52 Admiral Zumwalt
53 Actress Moore
55 Chicken's counterpart
56 Atmosphere: Prefix
57 Prefix with lateral
58 Omicrons' predecessors
59 Thesaurus listing: Abbr.

by Alex K. Justin

16

ACROSS
1 Play opening
5 Ran
9 Shawl or afghan
14 Forsaken
15 Yellow brick, e.g.
16 Moonshine
17 Unencumbered
19 Composed
20 Follower of 21-Across?
21 Follower of 20-Across?
22 Small: Suffix
23 Ripped
24 Dems. opposition
27 Proverbial distancer
32 Sleepy Hollow schoolmaster
34 Ampersand
35 Firpo of the ring
36 Folk tales
37 Ship's officers
39 ___ time (never)
40 Upshots
41 Morning hrs.
42 Waffle topping
43 Kind of disease, facetiously
47 Hook shape
48 Alphabet quartet
49 Unmixed, as a drink
51 Character actor George
54 Starts
58 In the thick of
59 Be afraid to offend
60 Hope of Hollywood
61 Manhattan campus
62 Gamblers' game
63 Boorish
64 Some combos
65 Sharp put-down

DOWN
1 ___ Romeo (automobile)
2 Hip
3 De ___ (too much)
4 Words before "red" or "running"
5 Literary sister
6 Give some slack
7 Maneuver slowly
8 White House monogram
9 Block
10 Fun and games
11 Kind of beer
12 Eight, in combinations
13 A question of time
18 Singer Lenya
21 Merchandise
23 Manner of speaking
24 Staff leader
25 University of Maine site
26 TV announcer Don
28 1980 DeLuise movie
29 Bizarre
30 "Peanuts" character
31 Stock plans providing worker ownership: Abbr.
33 Young 'uns
37 Horace and Thomas
38 BB's
42 Disreputable
44 Some are spitting
45 World cultural agcy.
46 Flirts
50 Stylish Brits
51 Baby powder
52 Poet Khayyám
53 ___ fide
54 Where humuhu-munuku-nukuapuaa might be served
55 Filly or colt
56 Roman marketplaces
57 Quit
59 Abbr. in a mail-order ad

by Ernie Furtado

ACROSS

1 Bakery byproduct
6 Went by plane
10 Copied
14 Arizona features
15 Scottish isle
16 Lemon's partner
17 With 36-Across and 55-Across, a sales pitch disclaimer
20 Baden-Baden and others
21 Shea team
22 Eastern V.I.P.
23 Mr. Caesar
24 Ship to ___
25 "Swan Lake," e.g.
29 Tiny bit
31 Not native
32 Printer's employee
33 Printer's measures
36 See 17-Across
39 His wife took a turn for the worse
40 Obsolescent piano key material
41 Bellini opera
42 Hoarder's cry
43 Telescopist's sighting
44 Strength
47 Opponent
48 Xerox competitor
49 "When I was ___ . . ."
51 In ___ of
55 See 17-Across
58 Person 'twixt 12 and 20
59 "The King and I" setting
60 Singer Cara
61 Misses the mark
62 Paddles
63 Waco locale

DOWN

1 Concert hall equipment
2 Harvest
3 Greek mountain
4 Wrestlers' needs
5 Type of cobra
6 Shot
7 Artist's pad?
8 Son of Seth
9 Revolutionary, e.g.
10 "Remember the ___"
11 Heartbroken swain
12 Leno, for one
13 Bucks and does
18 Give forth
19 Indian noblewoman
23 Feeling
24 Suffix with tip or dump
25 Get-out-of-jail money
26 In addition
27 Bit of fluff
28 Mr. Durocher
29 Harden
30 "Sure, why not?"
32 Borodin's "Prince ___"
33 To be, in Paree
34 Secretarial work
35 Burn
37 Confess
38 "___ on your life!"
43 Fashion
44 "60 Minutes" regular
45 Reason out
46 Sentence subjects
47 Country homes
48 Pigeon coop
49 ___ da capo
50 Noted James Earl Jones stage role
51 Entice
52 The holm oak
53 Erupter of 1669
54 Applications
56 G.I. entertainers
57 Command to Fido

by Sidney L. Robbins

18

ACROSS
1 Artistic skill
6 Card game also called sevens
12 Holed out in two under par
14 Warned
16 English essayist Richard
17 Burglar
18 Cools, as coffee
19 Pumpkin eater of rhyme
21 Summer drink
22 Employee health plan, for short
23 Horse trainer's equipment
25 Black cuckoos
26 Long, long time
28 Like some schools
29 Sweetens the kitty
30 Smart alecks
32 Traffic circle
33 Charlie Brown's "Darn!"
34 Ex-Mrs. Burt Reynolds
35 Charge with gas
38 Adorned
42 Vineyard fruit
43 Kismet
44 Snick's partner
45 Detest
46 Alternative to eggdrop
48 A Gershwin
49 Drunk ___ skunk
50 Analyze a sentence
51 Actor John of TV's "Addams Family"
53 Locale
55 Money-back deal
57 Boot camp denizen
58 Noted family in china manufacture
59 Arabs
60 Cancel the launch

DOWN
1 "L'état ___": Louis XIV
2 Army grub
3 Ripening agent
4 Butler's "The Way of All ___"
5 ___ Aviv
6 Observed Lent
7 Change the hemline
8 ___-do-well
9 "La-la" preceder
10 Home of the '96 Olympics
11 Poorer
13 Arranges strategically
15 Smart
18 Sullivan's "really big" one
20 Summers, in Haiti
24 Sharp
25 Clowning achievements?
27 Mexican shawl
29 Top-flight
31 Arena receipts
32 Drive in Beverly Hills
34 Epistles
35 Shocked
36 Pencil ends
37 Knocking sound
38 Forbids
39 Bootee maker
40 Most Halloweenlike
41 Doyen
43 Smithies
46 Dwindled
47 High-muck-a-muck
50 Fir
52 Prefix with masochism
54 Item of office attire
56 Fuel efficiency rater: Abbr.

by William P. Baxley

ACROSS

1 One who reunes
5 Bic or Parker products
9 Lox's partner
14 Computer offering
15 Face shape
16 Shade of white
17 No ifs, ___ or buts
18 Soho so-long
19 Lounges lazily
20 Start of a quip
23 Consumed
24 Israeli airport
25 ___ chango (magician's command)
29 "That was close!"
31 Horror film frightener
34 Oscar de la ___
35 Mimi Sheraton subject
36 Obstinate one
37 Middle of the quip
40 Hor.'s opposite
41 ___ of March
42 French avenue
43 It's north of Calif.
44 Chance ___ (meet accidentally)
45 Not present
46 Columbus univ.
47 One, in Orléans
48 End of the quip
55 His beloved was Beatrice
56 Old newspaper section
57 Hide
59 Rags-to-riches writer
60 Roughneck
61 Bombeck, the columnist
62 Hops brews
63 Sea eagle
64 Cooper's was high

DOWN

1 Internists' org.
2 Give temporarily
3 Remove, as a knot
4 Daydream
5 Spud
6 Dodge
7 European defense grp.
8 Dross
9 Swell, as a cloud
10 Have nothing to do with
11 Course game
12 A Gardner
13 Fleur-de-___
21 Old Nick
22 Coasters
25 Utah city
26 Allude (to)
27 ___ nous
28 Editor's mark
29 Part of NOW
30 Breaks up clods
31 Company B awakener
32 ". . . in tears amid the ___ corn": Keats
33 Ism
35 Rover's playmate
36 Tormé and Gibson
38 Raise the end of
39 Cacophonous tower
44 Does a groomsman's job
45 Whosoever
46 Bewhiskered animal
47 Author Sinclair
48 Fabric texture
49 "Come Back Little Sheba" playwright
50 Prod
51 Rating a D
52 Aboveboard
53 Florida's Beach
54 Pollster Roper
55 A tiny bit
58 Ecru

by Betty Jorgensen

20

ACROSS

1 Expire, as a membership
6 Show hosts, for short
9 Fill
13 Secretary of State Root
14 Dadaist Hans
15 Like Old King Cole
16 Baseball bigwig Bud
17 Assurance
19 Not brand-name
21 Spring blooms
22 Wildebeest
23 Entomological stage
25 Less original
28 Monks and nuns
32 Apartment sign
33 Lebanese symbol
34 Soup container
35 Immense, poetically
36 Mine find
37 Lift the spirits of
39 From ___ Z
40 Most Egyptians
42 Meet official
43 Louvre highlight
45 Insult
46 1983 Streisand role
47 Scottish denial
48 Value
51 Lethargy
55 Prohibition establishment
57 Chain of hills
59 Country music's Tucker
60 Drunk's problem, with "the"
61 Near Eastern chieftain
62 Bettor's starter
63 Opposite of WNW
64 Pores over

DOWN

1 Broadway's "___ Miz"
2 Words after shake or break
3 Mass
4 Roof worker
5 Noted name in puzzling
6 Biblical trio
7 Fancy term for 5-Down and 15-Down
8 Vacation destination
9 Grad-to-be
10 Liberal ___
11 Corner
12 Potato features
15 Noted name in puzzling
18 Lasso
20 Capek play
24 Styles
25 It may come in a head
26 Kemo Sabe's companion
27 Crazy as ___
29 "___, I saw . . ."
30 Eroded
31 Dummy Mortimer
33 Slide
38 Cable choice
41 Washer cycle
44 "Roger," at sea
45 ___ for the books
48 Film dog
49 Breadth
50 Faxed
52 Wall Street abbr.
53 Brainstorm
54 Like some cheeses
56 Suffix added to fruit names
58 Speech stumbles

by Martin Schneider

ACROSS
1 Tops of wine bottles
6 Wreak havoc upon
12 Gorge
13 Undergoes again, as an experience
14 Fund-raiser
15 Requiring immediate action
16 Postprandial drinks
18 Dessert pastry
19 ___ hurrah
20 Actor Jannings
22 Chest rattle
23 Brightened
25 Burghoff role on "M*A*S*H"
27 Columbia, vis-à-vis the ocean
28 Entraps
30 Nullifies
32 Hash house sign
34 Info
35 Reduces
38 Glass ingredient
42 Tex-___ (hot cuisine)
43 DeMille films
45 Exorcist's adversary
46 Elderly
48 Angry to-do
49 Cable TV's C-___
50 Scuttlebutt
52 Take to court
55 Burst inward
57 Aficionado
58 It stretches across a tennis court
59 Bellyached
60 They may be liquid
61 Tried to catch a conger

DOWN
1 Variety of rummy
2 William Tell and others
3 Prevalent
4 Make a sweater
5 Hunting dog
6 Tyrannosaurus ___
7 Parted company with a horse
8 Good physical health
9 Nothing special
10 Calms
11 Hold in high regard
12 Stay
13 Sojourned
14 Strike alternatives
17 Muscat is its capital
21 Former capital of Nigeria
24 "___-porridge hot . . ."
26 Word before fire or transit
29 Hitchcock's "The Thirty-Nine ___"
31 Hubble, e.g.
33 Cut, as roses
35 Peanuts, e.g.
36 Frees from liability
37 Disfigure
39 Ascribed
40 Like nuts at a chocolatier's
41 French year
42 Boater's haven
44 Plodding person
47 Fellini's "La ___ Vita"
51 Cheer (for)
53 Devoid of moisture
54 The dark force
56 O.R. personnel

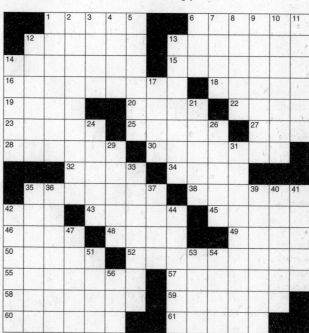

by Nancy Joline

22

ACROSS

1 Like some eagles or tires
5 Poker Flat chronicler
10 Price
14 "Now ___ me down . . ."
15 Dillies
16 Patron saint of physicians
17 In need
19 "Miss ___ Regrets"
20 Former Washington nine
21 Journalists Joseph and Stewart
23 Bog
24 Dutch painter Jan
25 Actor Peter
28 Fleet cats
31 Comic Costello
32 ___ incognita
34 Psalms word
35 "Bon" words
37 Appears
39 Flintstones pet
40 Bit of clowning
42 Soup ingredients
44 Cattle call
45 Newborns
47 Shortly
49 End of a tunnel, proverbially
50 Came in horizontally
51 Manhandler
53 Fellow crew member
57 Have an itch for
58 "Fantastic!"
60 1949 hit "___ in Love With Amy"
61 Sky-hued flower

62 Shoe support
63 Glassmaker's oven
64 Broadcasts
65 Asserts

DOWN

1 Invitations
2 A lily
3 Mowing site
4 Ball of fire
5 Feted ones
6 Tennis's Agassi
7 Collectors' cars
8 Robert Morse stage role
9 Subject of a will
10 Shut up
11 In a tenuous position
12 Leave hastily
13 1994 film "Guarding ___"

18 Like Pisa's tower
22 Sediment
24 Humiliate
25 Broadway tune "___ River"
26 Ten-___ odds
27 Not with it
28 Northern Indians
29 Vietnam's capital
30 "Darn it!"
33 Rent out again
36 Presaging trouble
38 One-way transporters
41 Zoo fixture
43 Cuts
46 Pulses
48 Owns up to
50 Protected, as the feet

51 Subject to court-martial, maybe
52 Curse
53 Bedaze
54 Taj Mahal site
55 "___ also serve who . . ."
56 Hot times on the Riviera
59 Little: Suffix

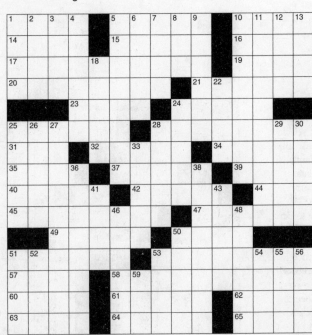

by Bernice Gordon

ACROSS

1 Outbuildings
6 Hobgoblin
10 "___ sesame"
14 Mischievous sprite
15 Selves
16 Nuclear reactor
17 Ahead of the times
19 Prefix with marketing
20 Sleep stage
21 Accurate
22 Made an incursion
24 Medicine that's not all it's promised to be
26 Bewails
27 Fictitious
30 Trigonometric function
32 Sashes
33 Oil city of Iran
34 Memorable period
37 Melts
40 It may be penciled in
42 Ott or Gibson
43 Appraised
45 Inland sea east of the Caspian
46 Rephrased
48 Lord Peter Wimsey's creator
50 Caper
52 Uproar
54 Evades
56 ___ of arms
57 Small amount
60 Woodwind instrument
61 Restaurant special
64 Add-on
65 Swearword
66 Valletta is its capital
67 Not the pictures
68 Nautical chains
69 Stocking material

DOWN

1 Box
2 Busy place
3 Word with eye or final
4 Gunga ___
5 Resolve
6 ___ Arts
7 Monstrously cruel
8 The Almighty
9 River to the North Sea
10 Right to purchase
11 Secondary residence
12 Actress Burstyn
13 Desiderata
18 Electric power network
23 Astound
24 Noted lioness
25 Take new vows
27 Froth
28 French ecclesiastic
29 Love letter
31 Low island
33 Fall bloomer
35 Bellow
36 Piercing tools
38 Instant
39 ___ one's words
41 Reddish-brown horses
44 Give a little learning
47 Reader's ___
48 Miner's nail
49 Cooling-off time
50 Take as one's own
51 Aristocratic
53 Closet pests
55 Espy
57 Kewpie, e.g.
58 Prefix with graph or crat
59 Breakfast fiber source
62 Ballad
63 Blue bird

by James L. Beatty

ACROSS

1 Mosque tops
6 Lone Ranger attire
10 Strike caller
13 Dynamic
14 "I cannot tell ___"
15 Mimic
16 Chinese principles
18 Lavish party
19 Tosspot
20 Worships
21 Freshly
22 Life, for one
23 Enlarge
24 Soup dipper
28 Six-stanza poem
31 Lily
32 Does, for example
33 Knot of hair
36 Procrastinator
40 Relative of the buttercup
42 Moral no-no
43 Tentmaker of fame
45 Kind of camera focus
46 Modified
49 Mount
50 Sighed (for)
52 Playboy pic
54 Took a taxi
55 Sound choice?
57 Busy person around Apr. 15
60 Smidgen that's smashed
61 Occasionally
63 Greek letters
64 Kurdish home
65 Throw out
66 N.Y. winter time
67 Trapper's trophy
68 Fires

DOWN

1 TV's "___ of Our Lives"
2 Hodgepodge
3 Money maker
4 "Uncle Tom's Cabin" girl
5 Spot for 100
6 Giuliani and others
7 Equipped with a theft protector
8 Trig function
9 Barrels
10 No longer bedridden
11 Fracas
12 Shrimp
15 Once more
17 Successor to H.S.T.
23 Telegram
24 Lassies' partners
25 Jai ___
26 Homeless
27 Conducted
29 Melville novel setting
30 Countdown start
34 "Render therefore ___ Caesar . . ."
35 It's a gas
37 Trucker's amount
38 Holy Roman, e.g.: Abbr.
39 Squealer
41 Alluring West
44 License extension
47 Considers
48 "The Story of Civilization" author
49 Hollow stones
50 Jabber
51 Specks
53 Bear's abode
55 Quick cut
56 Ripped
57 In high style
58 Captain Ahab film
59 Busy ones
62 Initials of 1933

by Sidney L. Robbins

ACROSS

1 "___ Without a Cause"
6 Musical scale letters
11 Joker
14 Smell
15 Of great scope
16 Electric ___
17 Proverb
18 Old-fashioned picture taker
20 Elevator name
22 Victory symbol
23 Norse Zeus
24 Candidate Landon
26 Was sore
28 Having divergent lines
29 Backside
31 DNA shapes
33 Letter getter
35 Seize
36 That lady
39 Make into a spiral
40 Book after Deuteronomy
42 Opposite SSW
43 ___ Mahal
45 12, at dice
46 Leisurely study
48 Eric of "Monty Python"
49 October gems
52 ___ Rouge
54 Olive ___
55 Sushi go-with
56 National anthem contraction
57 Author Irwin
59 Intercom
62 Smoldering spark
65 Unfashionable
66 "___ a Rainy Night" (1981 hit)
67 On top of
68 Formerly named
69 One of life's certainties, in a saying
70 Deep-___ (discarded)

DOWN

1 Type of computer chip
2 Historical time
3 Ticket booth
4 Discharge
5 Keats poem
6 Recede
7 Beg shamelessly
8 Trapped
9 European freshwater fish
10 Medicine watchdog: Abbr.
11 Uncared-for, as a lawn
12 Eagle's nest
13 Liver or thyroid
19 Extinct birds
21 Rhodes ___
24 Jingle writers
25 Greg Evans cartoon
27 Use voodoo on
28 Crate up again
30 ___ Jo, of the '88 Olympics
32 Coaxes
34 Mosquito marks
36 Train for the ring
37 ___-burly
38 Artist's prop
41 ___-fi
44 Diner music maker
45 "Kapow!"
46 Entreaty
47 ___ Tuesday
49 Director Welles
50 Irritate
51 Not obtuse
53 Three-toed birds
56 Neighbor of Ark.
58 Both: Prefix
60 Acumen
61 Illiterates' signatures
63 The day before
64 Ruby

by Ed Pegg Jr.

26

ACROSS

1 ". . . more than one way to skin ___"
5 Supply a party
10 Beast of burden
13 Fads
15 Speak publicly
16 Caltech rival
17 Cereal "fruit"
19 "___ of these days, Alice . . ."
20 Outdoor
21 Spiritual punishment
23 Meadow
24 Jockey Cordero
25 Civil War flash point
32 Nom de crook
33 Upset
34 Small dog, for short
37 Split
38 Grew ashen
40 Coffee, informally
41 Hat-room fixture
42 Salon offering
43 More painful
44 U.S. commodore in Japan, 1853–54
47 Letter-shaped metal bar
50 Señor Guevara
51 Lovebirds' destination, maybe
54 Paul of "Casablanca"
59 ___ Altos, Calif.
60 County of Northern Ireland
62 Had a little lamb?
63 First name in cosmetics
64 Novelist Françoise
65 Roll of bills
66 Looks (to be)
67 Unattached

DOWN

1 With the bow, in music
2 Bellyache
3 Malarial symptom
4 Part of T.V.A.: Abbr.
5 Hooded snakes
6 Exist
7 Diamond cover
8 To be, to Satie
9 "___ the Fox" (classic fable)
10 In the midst of
11 From the time of
12 Girder material
14 ___ of justice
18 Yesterday: Fr.
22 "___ luck?"
25 David's instrument
26 Downwind, nautically
27 Wedding sine qua non
28 Add to, unnecessarily
29 Smut
30 Prior to, in poems
31 Crimson
34 Henry VIII's VIth
35 "Reply completed," to a ham operator
36 Queen of Scots
38 Word before bull or stop
39 Grasshopper's rebuker
40 Baseball's DiMaggio
42 Mexican snacks
43 Isn't miserly
44 Cosmo, e.g.
45 Reverberations
46 At what time?
47 Wedding acquisition
48 Flora and fauna
49 Let up
52 Type of wine
53 Kitty starter
55 Kind of estate
56 Therefore
57 Major rug exporter
58 Unit of force
61 Rep. foe

by Jonathan Schmalzbach

ACROSS

1 Room between rooms
5 Handouts
9 Farm building
13 Opera solos
15 West Virginia resource
16 Sack starter
17 1970 Tommy Roe hit
20 Spain's locale
21 Leslie Caron role
22 Hesitation sounds
23 Writer Bombeck
25 Swindle
26 Sweet treat
30 "Fiddler on the Roof" fellow
35 Literary collection
36 Weep loudly
37 Arctic, for one
38 Recurring theme
41 French denial
43 Lisboa's sister city
44 1985 Kate Nelligan title role
45 Big shot
47 Calendar ender: Abbr.
48 Anglo's partner
49 Tentacled sea creature
52 Ostrich's cousin
54 Author Bellow
55 Lemon drink
58 Meadow bird
60 Drinkers' toasts
64 "Black Bottom Stomp" performer
67 Came down
68 Christmas centerpiece
69 The elder Judd
70 Critic Rex
71 Cruising
72 Tiff

DOWN

1 Pilgrim to Mecca
2 Pilgrim to Mecca
3 Citrus flavor
4 Emblem of victory
5 Item up the sleeve
6 Take it easy
7 Slander
8 With cunning
9 Visit Vail, perhaps
10 "Come Back, Little Sheba" playwright
11 Cowardly Lion portrayer
12 Chooses
14 Helical
18 Doorway parts
19 Perfect
24 Long, long time
26 Caan or Cagney
27 ___ Gay
28 Type of rubber
29 Superior to
31 Author Umberto
32 "Rigoletto" composer
33 Film director Peter
34 Tennyson's "___ Arden"
39 Odysseus's rescuer, in myth
40 Exquisitely
42 Guitarist Lofgren
46 Ecto or proto ending
49 Panel of 12
50 Alaskan river
51 Groups of indigenous plants
53 "I Remember Mama" mama
55 Partly open
56 Take out of print
57 Nobelist Wiesel
59 "Red Balloon" painter
61 On
62 ___ Linda, Calif.
63 Fit of anger
65 Former Ford
66 ___ & Perrins

by Raymond Hamel

28

ACROSS

1 Gregory Hines specialty
4 Take for granted
10 Colorless
14 Actress Gardner
15 Stay-at-home
16 Roof overhang
17 House member: Abbr.
18 Interior decorator's hiree
20 Wields the gavel
22 Swear (to)
23 Pinker inside
24 Opponent
25 Greek geometer
27 Premolar
31 Pallid
32 Secrete
33 Poi ingredient
34 Fed. power agcy.
35 Diffidence
38 Sword's superior, in saying
39 Craving
41 Ends' partner
42 More than fat
44 Stereo components
46 32-card card game
47 Effect a makeover
48 Napoleon's cavalry commander
49 Slow, in music
52 Bring an issue home
55 Pet rock, maybe
57 Hair application
58 Formerly
59 Mother __
60 The 90's, e.g.
61 Goes out with regularly
62 Archeological finds
63 Director Howard

DOWN

1 Canvas cover
2 Declare positively
3 Houseman TV series, with "The"
4 Two are often prescribed
5 Under the elms
6 "Great!"
7 Salt Lake City team
8 Russian for "peace"
9 Makes more valuable
10 Person who's feeling down in the mouth?
11 Fad
12 Lexington and Madison: Abbr.
13 Lahr or Parks
19 One of the Aleutians
21 Shopper's lure
24 Adjutants
25 Noblemen
26 Exhaust
27 Ties
28 Toothless threat
29 "__ my case"
30 Gift recipient
32 Kind of power
36 Barn dances
37 Legendary hemlock drinker
40 Sidewinder lock-ons
43 False god
45 Actor Dullea
46 A form of 46-Across
48 Tycoon
49 Primates
50 Madonna's "Truth or __"
51 Church area
52 Lo-cal
53 Mr. Mostel
54 Flair
56 Chow down

by Robert Zimmerman

29

ACROSS

1 Fitzgerald's forte
5 Shortening
9 "___ little piggy . . ."
13 Impetuous
14 Sunburn remedy
15 Rule the ___
16 Agitate
17 Have on
18 Simone's school
19 Epithet for a TV set
22 Jeanne or Thérèse: Abbr.
23 Believer in God
24 Podunk
30 Eucharistic plate
31 Lascivious looks
32 Set-to
35 On ___ with (equal to)
36 High in pitch
37 Mongol monk
38 Bandman Brown
39 Baseball's Doubleday
41 Bank patron
42 Fixation
44 "Queenie" author Michael
46 Get a move on
47 Gambler's tormentor
53 Beau ___
54 Flub
55 Eye layer
57 Take back to the car pound
58 Axlike tool
59 60's vocalist Vikki
60 German river
61 "Let's Make a Deal" choice
62 Make a cable stitch

DOWN

1 Last year's jrs.
2 Marcus Porcius
3 M ___ Mary
4 Farm machine
5 Maker of cases
6 Not aweather
7 Abbey or Tobacco, e.g.
8 Suffix for 41-Down
9 Alarm bell
10 Catcalls
11 Wee atoll
12 Ending for hip or hoop
15 Extends a subscription
20 School founded in 1440
21 Fragrance
24 October birthstone
25 Place for a necklace clasp
26 Hellenic H's
27 Obliqueness
28 Moray pursuer
29 Aquarium fish
32 Sitarist Shankar
33 Bodement
34 Voting district
37 Politician with a limited future
39 Hurricane of 1992
40 Smile broadly
41 Word before deep or dive
42 Demosthenes, e.g.
43 Impatient one
44 Bumped impolitely
45 Spanish direction
47 Grimm villain
48 "Yipes!"
49 Old fogy
50 Dolt
51 Netman Lendl
52 Garr of "Tootsie"
56 Trump's "The ___ of the Deal"

by John Greenman

ACROSS

1 Bend
5 Exchange
9 Polite form of address
13 Actor Calhoun
14 Make ___ for (argue in support of)
15 Ray of Hollywood
16 This puzzle's mystery subject
19 "The Joy Luck Club" author
20 Fuzzy
21 Rule
22 Yield
23 Dubbed one
24 1951 movie with 16-Across
31 Stumble
32 River to the Caspian
33 Veterans Day mo.
35 Daly of "Gypsy"
36 Competition for Geraldo
38 Trig function
39 Wynken, Blynken and ___
40 They're sometimes wild
41 Earth mover
42 1957 movie with 16-Across
47 Thumbnail sketch
48 16-Across's "Cat on ___ Tin Roof"
49 Étagère piece
52 County north of San Francisco
54 Neighbor of Ind.
57 1946 movie with 16-Across
60 "___ known then what . . ."

61 Cancel
62 "A" code word
63 Greek portico
64 Use épées
65 Half a fortnight

DOWN

1 Stew
2 "Damn Yankees" seductress
3 Green land
4 ___ Affair
5 Play's start
6 He coined the term "horsepower"
7 Pallid
8 Caress
9 M-G-M's Louis B, and others
10 "___ know is what . . ."
11 Sick as ___

12 Dawn
14 Put up with
17 Novelist Waugh
18 Disney mermaid
22 Horn, for one
23 Iranian chief, once
24 Letter abbr.
25 Richard of "Bustin' Loose"
26 Newswoman Ellerbee
27 Tend to
28 Refrain syllable
29 Confederacy's opponent
30 Three trios
34 Exceedingly
36 Eight: Prefix
37 Through
38 Latched

40 Law professor Hill
43 Airline to Spain
44 Outpouring of gossip
45 Bit of fall weather
46 Miss O'Neill
49 Publisher Adolph
50 Sloop
51 Defense means
52 Diner's guide
53 First-class
54 Man or Ely, e.g.
55 16-Across's "___ With Father"
56 Plumber's concern
58 Travel (about)
59 16-Across's "The Last Time I ___ Paris"

by Bette Sue Cohen

ACROSS

1 Interlaced
6 Canadian tree
11 Unit of chewing tobacco
14 Idiotic
15 Relieve
16 One of Frank's exes
17 Motion picture award
19 ___ Kippur
20 ___ ex machina
21 Red Square figure
23 Spacecraft sections
27 Tentative forays
29 Gone from the program
30 Shoulders-to-hips areas
31 "___ Irish Rose"
32 Paper purchases
33 Once existed
36 Guitarist Lofgren
37 See 30-Down
38 ___ fide
39 Farm enclosure
40 Crude characters
41 Gershwin hero
42 Jai alai ball
44 "Ode to ___ Joe"
45 Votes
47 Hamlet, at times
48 Shrine to remember
49 Spotted
50 Reunion-goers
51 Nature personified
58 First lady
59 "Middlemarch" author
60 Inventor Howe

61 Matched grouping
62 Tears
63 Show shock, e.g.

DOWN

1 Store-bought hair
2 Musician Yoko
3 Actor Kilmer
4 Football lineman
5 Tries to rile
6 John Fowles novel, with "The"
7 "___ Well That Ends Well"
8 Hebron grp.
9 Big, friendly dog, for short
10 Huxley's "___ in Gaza"
11 Teen film hit of 1992

12 To have, to Héloïse
13 Curses
18 Require
22 "Xanadu" musical grp.
23 Signifies
24 Pluto's path
25 Perry's paper
26 Functions
27 Bubble masses
28 Columnist Bombeck
30 With 37-Across, the ground
32 Wild times
34 1973 Rolling Stones hit
35 Word with nay or sooth
37 Bit of poetry
38 Manila machete
40 Early feminist

41 Avant-gardist
43 Slippery ___
44 Rabbit's title
45 Hardens, as clay
46 Breathing
47 Borscht ingredients
49 Bullet-riddled
52 Cheer
53 Malleable metal
54 Pale or Newcastle brown
55 Narrow inlet
56 Middle X or O
57 Presidential initials

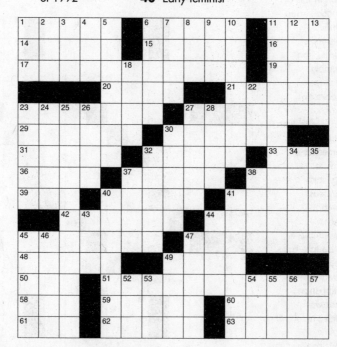

by Wayne Robert Williams

32

ACROSS

1 Unhappy
5 Man with the world on his shoulders
10 Israeli carrier
14 "Mona ___"
15 Scarlett's love
16 Comic Rudner
17 What we celebrate on July 4
20 Honor, with "to"
21 Form 1040 amount
22 Buntline and Rorem
23 Sean Connery, e.g.
24 Duke's home
27 Fifth Avenue name
28 Catch in the act
31 Gaucho's rope
32 Golfer Ballesteros
33 Old Russian assembly
34 What we observe on July 4
37 Bronze and Iron
38 Some intersections
39 Think
40 Stag party attendees
41 Scorch
42 Ranch
43 Tools locale
44 ___ de foie gras
45 Book after Nehemiah
48 Fortification
52 What we watch on July 4
54 A lulu
55 Miss Brooks portrayer
56 Muck
57 Witnessed
58 Stocking material
59 Some whiskies

DOWN

1 Happy
2 Green shade
3 Employed
4 Seasons, as meat
5 Teen hangout
6 Dean Martin's "___ Amore"
7 ___ majesté
8 Arm of the Treasury Dept.
9 Ill
10 Construct
11 Island near Venice
12 Mighty mite
13 Costly cloth
18 Hangover soother?
19 Son of Seth
23 Baseball and hockey stats
24 Father of Hector and Paris
25 Denny of the N.B.A.
26 Weighed down
27 Passover feast
28 Blue entertainment
29 Hotpoint rival
30 Sang to the moon
32 Golf legend Sam
33 Doctor's instrument
35 Intangible
36 Egypt's ___ Church
41 "Good night, ___" (old TV phrase)
42 Briny
43 Like Samson, once
44 Kind of truck
45 Heroic poetry
46 "Auld Lang ___"
47 It's better known for its bark than its bite
48 Third degrees, usually
49 Seaman's shout
50 Nod off
51 Rams' dams
53 Dernier ___

by Joel Davajan

ACROSS

1 High rung on the evolutionary ladder
6 Alternative to a shower
10 Quatrain rhyme scheme
14 Like __ from the blue
15 Environs
16 Wise guy
17 Popular chocolate snack
19 On the level
20 River through Florence
21 Mother __
22 Help in crime
23 Quad number
24 Lock
25 Torah readers
29 Forgiving one
32 Oscar, e.g.
33 Prefix with cycle
34 Draft org.
37 March events?
40 Lolita
42 Phony prefix
43 Fond du __, Wis.
44 New Zealand native
45 Where Spain and Portugal are
48 Seasoning
49 Afterward
51 Kind of show
53 Singer Minnelli
54 Kick locale
56 Dumb __
60 Paid promotion: Abbr.
61 Give up hard drink?
63 Vegetarian's no-no
64 Sheltered
65 Similar
66 Wan
67 Lease
68 Little ones

DOWN

1 It's a laugh
2 "Deutschland __ Alles"
3 Daybreak
4 What's more
5 To the __ degree
6 Louisiana waterway
7 Bowers
8 Socials
9 Tortoise's competitor
10 Glaring
11 Place to have one's head examined
12 Bouts of chills
13 Borscht ingredients
18 Selves
23 Hoedown musician
24 Shortened
25 Criticizes
26 Not at home
27 Coming-of-age event
28 Cross-one's-heart garment
30 Play on words
31 Some
35 Dried
36 Agitate
38 Unit of corn
39 Phys. or chem.
41 Baby food
46 "Reds" star
47 Out of bed
48 Bygone
49 Andean animal
50 Gofers
52 Commencement
54 Box lightly
55 Patriot Nathan
56 It's full of baloney
57 Final notice
58 Roué
59 War deity
62 Hardly an underperformer

by Sidney L. Robbins

34

ACROSS
1 Comic Martha
5 Bamboozle
9 Stoppers
14 Height: Abbr.
15 Face-to-face exam
16 Beau at the balcony
17 Town near Caen
18 Chockablock
20 Headlong
22 Resident's suffix
23 Race tracks
24 Dormitory din
28 Castle features
30 Offspring, genealogically: Abbr.
31 Celtic Neptune
32 Centers
33 Walk-on
34 Chancellorsville victor
35 Western Indian
36 Enmity
38 Sugar suffix
39 Singer Tillis
40 Word after many or honey
41 Conflict in Greek drama
42 French dance
43 A.L. or N.L. honorees
44 "Phèdre" dramatist
46 Flummoxes
48 Spring fragrance
49 Picture blowup: Abbr.
50 Head count
53 Game of digs and spikes
57 Parts of pelvises
58 Greek poet saved by a dolphin
59 Fit

60 Oodles
61 Mississippi Senator ___ Lott
62 Branch headquarters?
63 "Auld Lang ___"

DOWN
1 Answer: Abbr.
2 Der ___ (Adenauer moniker)
3 Cowardly one
4 Changes with the times
5 Carpentry pins
6 Europe/Asia separator
7 Dark shadow
8 Building wing
9 1984 Goldie Hawn movie
10 Look threatening

11 Actress Thurman
12 Solidify
13 Our sun
19 Xmas tree trimming
21 Spoil
24 Interstate trucks
25 Without rhyme or reason
26 "Schindler's List" star Liam
27 Novelist Graham
28 Hitches, as a ride
29 Surpass at the dinner table
30 Natural alarm clocks
33 Hoofbeats
36 About to occur
37 Pulchritudinous
41 Gum arabic trees
44 Garden brook
45 Completely

47 Juicy fruit
48 Takes it easy
50 Contemporary dramatist David
51 King of the beasts
52 Deceased
53 Large tub
54 Hockey's Bobby
55 Golf-ball position
56 Prohibit

by Wayne Robert Williams

ACROSS

1 "Woe is me!"
5 Inn, informally
10 Dollop
14 Frolic
15 Title holder
16 Burt's ex
17 Jai ___
18 Former auto executive
20 Two-pointers
22 Differs
23 Saucer occupants, for short
24 Mozart's "___ fan tutte"
25 Ball girl
28 Vacation spot
30 "Jerusalem Delivered" poet
34 Border lake
35 Car in a procession
37 Spring mo.
38 West Point salutatorian, 1829
41 Language ending
42 Off course
43 City two hours south of Lillehammer
44 Spreads the word
46 Bit of voodoo
47 Grueling tests
48 Sword with a guard
50 Louis Freeh's org.
51 Rubbed
54 Ascendant
58 Two-time U.S. Open golf champion
61 Kind of shark
62 Suffix with buck
63 Pentax rival
64 Sicilian rumbler
65 Poet Robert ___ Warren
66 Exhausted
67 Sunup direction

DOWN

1 Bedouin
2 She gets what she wants
3 Amo, ___, amat
4 Modern film maker
5 Leaves in a hurry
6 Wows
7 Jet's heading
8 Mercury and Jupiter, e.g.
9 "Well done!"
10 Actress DeHaven
11 Places
12 ___ over lightly
13 Kind of crime
19 Mobile unit?
21 Season of l'année
24 Polish producer
25 Cap
26 Having an irregular edge
27 Defame
28 Boil
29 Military chaplain
31 Hot sauce
32 Word with cold or breathing
33 Chocolate snacks
35 Elevations: Abbr.
36 Remark
39 Hardly one with a lilting voice
40 Neoprimitive American artist
45 Unextinguished
47 Kimono sash
49 Paradises
50 Weather line
51 Keep time manually
52 "You are ___"
53 Ages and ages
54 Soon
55 Ninth Greek letter
56 Actress Woods and others
57 Pest
59 One who gets special treatment
60 W.W. II hero

by Albert J. Klaus

36

ACROSS

1 Say "I do" again
6 March starter
9 Diplomatic skills
14 Dwelling place
15 U.N. member
16 Honolulu hello
17 Scrabble, anagrams, etc.
19 Bottoms of graphs
20 Disney dog
21 Round table titles
22 Mosque chiefs
23 Ave. crossers
24 "I've been ___!"
25 City on the Brazos
27 Ear cleaner
29 ___ race (finished first)
30 Lived
33 Oaxaca waters
35 Dictionaries and thesauruses
37 Organic soil
38 Subject of this puzzle
39 Lockup
40 Preambles
42 "You ___ Have to Be So Nice"
43 "The Sultan of Sulu" author
44 Crooner Williams
45 Jokester's props
46 Nightclub bits
47 Tricia Nixon ___
48 New Deal org.
51 Move furtively
54 Barely open
56 Bewail
57 Start of the French workweek
58 Some of them are famous
60 Not ___ in the world
61 Prayer word
62 ___ nous
63 Ex-baseball commish Ueberroth
64 Light time
65 Lucy's landlady

DOWN

1 Singer Lou
2 Enemy vessel
3 THIS HERE IRON SENT
4 Whirlpool
5 B.A. or Ph.D.
6 Like August weather, perhaps
7 Client
8 Computer access codes
9 City vehicle
10 Battle depicted in "The Last Command"
11 Hip joint
12 Not us
13 Freshness
18 Quickly: Abbr.
24 Towel word
26 Connectors
28 Housebroken
29 Circumlocutory
30 Poet laureate, 1843–50
31 Similar
32 Mil. officer
33 ___ Romeo
34 Well-mannered
35 Incoherent speech
36 Off Broadway award
38 Is obstinate
41 More erratic
42 Humanitarian Dorothea
45 Where a cruise calls
46 Previn or Kostelanetz
47 Disk jockey Kasem
49 San Diego pro
50 Photographer Adams
51 Masher's comeuppance
52 Politico Clare Boothe ___
53 ___ the finish
55 Al Hirt hit
56 ___ Blanc
59 Itsy-bitsy

by Thomas W. Schier

ACROSS

1 Brazilian dance
6 Teen woe
10 Loot
14 "The Tempest" sprite
15 Avoid
16 Sherwood Anderson's "Winesburg, ___"
17 Letter turner
19 Home for some crocodiles
20 Crimson foes
21 Ones who brood
22 Sees socially
23 Artist Magritte
24 Measured (out)
25 Sir Isaac
29 Teeter
31 Singer Merman
32 Beauty's companion
33 Oklahoma city
36 Comedian Jerry
38 Neck artery
40 Tit for ___
41 Destroy for fun
43 Tip over
44 Storied Plaza girl
46 Alarms
47 Square, e.g.
48 Help in mischief
50 Makes a mess
51 Off base, maybe
52 Use a letter opener
56 Papal name
57 "Perils of Pauline" star
59 Otherwise
60 First name in mysteries
61 Movado rival
62 Not natural
63 Olympian's quest
64 You'll get a rise out of this

DOWN

1 Pack rat's motto
2 Asia's ___ Sea
3 60's fashion
4 Writer Hecht and others
5 Pie ___ mode
6 Wan
7 One-fifth of humankind
8 Goofy
9 Opposite WSW
10 "Moonlight," e.g.
11 Arkansas location
12 Felt below par
13 "Here ___!"
18 Invitation info
22 Ruin
23 Stylish desks
24 Tableland
25 Egg container
26 Ms. Kett of old comics
27 Executive branch
28 Part of ITT: Abbr.
30 Per
32 Women's support group?
34 Eat well
35 Puts two and two together
37 Admiral Perry victory site
39 W.W. II agcy.
42 Beach protector
45 Like an unpaid policy
46 Wall Street order
47 In a foxy way
49 Yawning?
50 Raced
51 Space prefix
52 Tree locale
53 Valentino co-star ___ Lee
54 Residents: Suffix
55 Not pictures
57 "___ o' My Heart"
58 Kind of humor

by Sidney L. Robbins

38

ACROSS
1 Protection in a purse
5 Start, as a trip
11 Actor Max ___ Sydow
14 Lawyer Dershowitz
15 Dragon's prey
16 Author Levin
17 Ex-heavyweight champ
19 Galley slave's tool
20 "___ been had!"
21 Bad grades
22 "Is that so?"
24 Colonist
26 Rock's ___ Vanilli
27 Brit. ref. work
28 Triangular-sailed ships
30 Pencil name
33 Hotel lobby
34 "Ich ___ ein Berliner"
36 "Famous" cookie man
37 Little bits
38 Dumb ox
39 Four-poster
40 Linen shades
41 Leafy shelter
42 Small seals
44 Journalist Nellie
45 Get rid of, in slang
46 Deejay's need
50 Los Angeles player
52 Orbit period
53 Lumberjack's tool
54 Singer ___ Rose
55 Noble acts
58 ___ time (golfer's starting point)
59 Niagara Falls craft?
60 "Java" player Al
61 "___ day now . . ."
62 The "E" of H.R.E.
63 Chocolate-covered morsels

DOWN
1 Baseball's Roger
2 Extant
3 Middy opponent
4 Epilogue
5 Ran the show
6 Almighty
7 Lobster eaters' accessories
8 Hubbub
9 Second drafts
10 Pew attachment
11 A concertmaster holds it
12 Kind of vaccine
13 Not any
18 Ambitionless one
23 Pub drink
25 Stocking parts
26 Yucatán people
28 Name in computer software
29 7D, e.g.
30 Early Beatles describer
31 "Rag Mop" brothers
32 Legendary bluesman
33 Onward
35 Neither's mate
37 It sometimes comes in bars
38 Cassidy portrayer William
40 Uganda airport
41 Boombox sound
43 Jazz date
44 Long-eared pooch
46 Witch, at times
47 Fine cloth
48 Strive
49 Schick et al.
50 Disk contents
51 The yoke's on them
52 Cosmonaut Gagarin
56 Dada founder
57 ___ Na Na

by Fred Piscop

ACROSS

1 Day in Hollywood
6 Like a V.P.
10 Hula hoops, mood rings, etc.
14 Live
15 Talk drunkenly
16 Revise
17 Like Macaulay Culkin, in a 1990 movie
19 Mr. Mostel
20 Diner signs
21 The Boston ___
23 Sense of self
24 ___ Moines
26 One of the Greats
28 Loathed
33 Zilch
34 Egyptian deity
35 Jeanne d'Arc and others: Abbr.
37 Asp
41 Straddler's spot
44 Ordinary talk
45 Roman "fiddler"
46 Composer Thomas
47 Western Indian
49 Hair curls
51 Cheerleader's prop
54 Kind of nut or brain
55 Live
56 Verne captain
59 Cut in a hurry
63 Poses
65 Intersection concern
68 Mound
69 Tickled-pink feeling
70 Declaim
71 Confederate
72 Paradise
73 Big books

DOWN

1 N.J. neighbor
2 Plow pullers
3 Abundant
4 Ratio words
5 Bleachers
6 Mary Kay of cosmetics
7 Hog filler?
8 Certain wrestle
9 Boring tool
10 Turk topper
11 Run like ___
12 Somber tune
13 Remained firm
18 Trypanosome carrier
22 Divide the pie
25 ___ fire (ignite)
27 Certain wallpaper design
28 Dewy
29 Eastern V.I.P.
30 Fuss
31 Finishes
32 Postpone
36 Not a one panel cartoon
38 Yawn inducer
39 Go into hysterics
40 Soft drinks
42 Pretend
43 "I'm telling the truth!"
48 Appear
50 Awkward bloke
51 Bygone title
52 Bay window
53 Kind of detector
57 Fine, temperature wise
58 Convex/concave molding
60 Dated hairdo
61 Did laps in the pool
62 Abhor
64 Mata Hari, e.g.
66 Hatcher
67 Favorable vote

by Sidney L. Robbins

ACROSS

1 Collectible coin
10 Mescal source
15 First efforts at compromise
16 Tied up
17 Communicate
18 Actor John
19 Broad beam
20 Plus
22 ___ cloth (lingerie fabric)
23 Togetherness
25 Astronaut's supply
27 Web-footed bird
30 Overweight one
32 Turntable extension
35 Kind of book
38 Part of a Clue accusation
40 Earthy deposits
41 Car job
42 Kingmaker
45 Old veterans' org.
46 Onetime record label
47 Bullion
49 Buddhist teaching
51 Sheet of rock
55 Some MOMA art
57 Sweetly, in music
60 Anne McCaffrey's dragon world
61 Conjointly
63 Bit of trouble
65 Novelist Wyndham ___
66 Transmit, as to a satellite
67 Whaler's spear
68 Oiler locale

DOWN

1 Scottish author James et al.
2 Brooks of "Spenser: For Hire"
3 Accept
4 Montmartre money
5 List shortener
6 Kirlian photography phenomenon
7 "Napoleon at Eylau" painter
8 Fugard play, with "A"
9 Favorite of Elizabeth
10 Like
11 Accelerator
12 It bit Marlon Brando
13 Blue vessel
14 Actress Purviance
21 Composed
24 In ___ signo vinces (ancient motto)
26 Belly
28 "My Man Godfrey" star
29 Come from ___
31 Island NE of Corsica
32 Torn-collage artist
33 Crucifix
34 Annihilated
36 Actress Sommer
37 Poetic adverb
39 Wrench user
43 Satcom co.
44 Politicked
48 Stopped
50 One of the Roman Fates
52 ___ Bismol
53 Introduction
54 ___ temps (interval): Fr.
55 "The Corn is Green" Oscar nominee
56 On the briny
58 Kind of following
59 Elbe feeder
62 Nationality ending
64 Medical grp.

by Raymond Hamel

ACROSS

1 ___ Rica
6 Job for Perry Mason
10 Career summary
14 Top grade
15 "___ We Got Fun?"
16 Son of Seth
17 Jockey's handful
18 Govt. agent
19 Mounties: Abbr.
20 Meaningful silence
23 Prominent features of Alfred E. Neuman
24 Carnaval site
25 Shrimpish
27 University of Maryland player
29 Stumble
32 Antigone's sister
35 Mongolian desert
36 The Monkees' "___ Believer"
37 1987 Edward James Olmos film
40 Actor Chaney
41 Miner profits?
42 Guinea pig or groundhog
43 Emily Dickinson's hometown
45 Air freshener scent
46 Nixon and Schroeder
47 Black-eyed item
48 Shows approval
52 Film in which Hayley Mills played twins
56 Ballet leap
58 One of the Menendez brothers
59 Gaucho gear
60 Elliptical
61 Look
62 Last word of fairy tales
63 Cravings
64 Flexible Flyer, for one
65 Press secretary Dee Dee

DOWN

1 ___ diem (seize the day)
2 Puccini product
3 More like a fox
4 Filament material
5 Org.
6 Tabby treat
7 "We ___ please"
8 Breeze
9 Mediterranean spouter
10 Against
11 Stimulus
12 Mix of westerns
13 Venomous viper
21 Debts
22 Greek vowel
26 It's south of Saudi Arabia
28 Sign a check
29 Stylish, in the 60's
30 Basque, e.g.
31 Hair splitter
32 Mallorca, por ejemplo
33 Lively dance
34 Whisky-vermouth cocktail
35 Mdse.
38 Place to meet following a tennis match
39 Pick out of a lineup
44 Mertz and Merman
45 Looked too soon
47 Cracker Jack bonus
49 Speechify
50 Library gadget
51 Trains, in a way
53 Cribbage counters
54 Asia's ___ Sea
55 Streetcar
56 "The ___ Luck Club"
57 Night before

by Julian Ochrymowych and Amy Goldstein

42

ACROSS

1 Hypothetical eccentricities in time
6 Competition
10 Jail unit
14 "___ man with seven wives"
15 Miss Cinders of old comics
16 Singer Guthrie
17 Brightly sunburned
19 Leaning
20 60's space chimp
21 Heroic legends
22 Teen woe
23 Beelzebub
24 Aware of
25 French painter Jean
29 Hesitation sounds
30 ___ di-dah
31 Sports sites
33 Mr. Whitney
35 Slippery one
38 Calms medically
40 Car gear
42 Mount St. Helens spew
43 "How dry ___"
44 Cylindrical
45 Self
47 Pass receiver
50 "M*A*S*H" character
51 Flake material
52 Boors
54 Cordial
55 They get smashed
56 Clumsy ships
60 One of five
61 Oscar winner for "Sayonara"
63 Lease
64 ___ Stanley Gardner
65 Boundary
66 Advantage
67 Philosopher A. J. ___
68 Versifiers

DOWN

1 Use Western Union
2 Prayer's closing
3 Effect a makeover
4 School orgs.
5 Airline to Stockholm
6 Cash back
7 Sour brew
8 Under-the-sink item
9 Sups
10 Poolside hut
11 Greenland settler
12 Grassy plain
13 Mislay
18 Botanist Gray
23 Depot
24 Hardy and North
25 Pedro's house
26 Silver holders
27 It misleads
28 Broadway's "Three Men ___ Horse"
32 Ocean
34 Permit
36 This, in Barcelona
37 Amorous gaze
39 Place of refinement
41 Baseball stat
46 Reproductive cell
48 Kind of soup
49 Not so clever
51 Exposed
53 Houston sch.
54 Had been
55 Length × width, for a rectangle
56 Prefix with sphere
57 Judicial cover?
58 Mend, as bones
59 Speedy planes
62 Spigot

by Sidney L. Robbins

ACROSS

1 Impudent youngster
6 Salesmen, briefly
10 Impudent talk
14 Cheapskate
15 Beasts of burden
16 Baseball's ___ brothers
17 1994 film role for Jim Carrey
19 Movers' trucks
20 More like winter sidewalks
21 Singer Estefan
23 Inge play
26 Closet spook
28 Nabokov novel
29 Clique
31 Norse deity
32 Film maker Wertmuller
34 Window surrounding
36 Fiery gems
41 Photographer's instruction
44 Rob
45 Neophyte
46 Paradise
47 Wedding vow
49 Soak (up)
51 Actor Tognazzi
52 By airmail from France
57 Dealer in cloth
59 "___ Twist"
60 England's Scilly ___
62 Call to the phone
63 Happy camper?
68 Kuwaiti honcho
69 Nile queen, for short
70 Neutral shade
71 Does lawnwork
72 Bakery bite
73 Of the eyes

DOWN

1 New Deal grp.
2 Sot's interjection
3 Just manage, with "out"
4 Writer Ira of "Sliver"
5 Concise summary
6 Old-fashioned learning method
7 Long-distance commuter's home
8 For each
9 Full of obstacles
10 "Stompin' at the ___"
11 Wake-up noise
12 Actress Braga
13 "Black-eyed" girl
18 Most hospitable
22 "Vive ___!" (old Parisian cry)
23 Becomes tiresome
24 Ninny
25 Tippy transportation
27 Those not mentioned
30 Arm art
33 Letters before an alias
35 Not outgoing
37 Leading prefix
38 Make sense
39 Feudal lord
40 Man of the casa
42 ___ and kicking
43 Bribe money
48 Straightforward
50 Magician's word
52 Vatican leaders
53 Texas shrine
54 Strict
55 Declares
56 Neighbor of Chad
58 Songwriters' grp.
61 Tab's target
64 Pie ___ mode
65 No longer chic
66 Wire service
67 Old-time gumshoe

by Wayne Robert Williams

44

ACROSS

1 Extreme point in an orbit
6 "Hogan's Heroes" extra
10 Cole ___
14 Hayes's predecessor
15 Arabian sultanate
16 ___ colada
17 Cecil B. DeMille epic, with "The"
20 Prohibition oasis?
21 Pilgrim John
22 What a ring lacks
23 "Finally!"
24 On ship
28 Plate scrapings
29 In a moment
30 Peculiar
32 Fast plane
35 English-French conflict beginning 1337
39 Greek vowel
40 Bay window
41 Prefix with pilot
42 "Scram!"
43 Went in a hurry
45 South American plains
48 Shock
50 ___ acid
51 Jerk
56 What 17-Across had
58 Tooth pain
59 Los Angeles 11
60 Skater's figure
61 "The ___ the limit"
62 Relative of the heckelphone
63 Teacher's charge

DOWN

1 10-percenters: Abbr.
2 Get ready, informally
3 Of sound mind
4 Native Peruvian
5 "Dracula" author Bram
6 Wanderer
7 Gather
8 Wacky
9 Neither Rep. nor Dem.
10 Takes part in a bee
11 One of the McCartneys
12 Opening bets
13 Jimmy Dorsey's "___ It You?"
18 Repair
19 Make a difference
23 Sills song
24 Late tennis V.I.P.
25 Title ___
26 Mrs. Chaplin
27 Also
28 Pitcher Hershiser
30 Revise copy
31 Potato feature
32 Done laps
33 Surfeit
34 Trampled
36 Florid
37 Times to write about
38 ___ Paulo, Brazil
42 Treats with malice
43 Bantu people
44 "Just a moment . . ."
45 Drug-yielding plants
46 "Alas and ___"
47 Netted
48 Sad sack
49 The ones over there
51 Knife
52 Drop in a letter box
53 Actress Swenson
54 Old English letters
55 Beach-storming vessels: Abbr.
57 To and ___

by Sidney L. Robbins

ACROSS
1 Adam and Eve locale
5 Pecan or poplar
9 Track official
14 Fully cooked
15 Do damage to
16 Become used (to)
17 Chew like a beaver
18 Radiate
19 Out of practice
20 Popular topping
22 Fire-gone conclusion
23 Film extras?
24 German-Polish border river
25 Industrial tub
26 Buttermilk's rider
28 Metal-in-the-rough
31 Comfortably inviting
34 Thick strings
35 Fix a squeak
36 Prayer ending
37 Mock-innocent query
38 Some med. insurance cos.
39 ___ good turn (help)
40 Suspicious
41 "All That Jazz" director Bob
42 Write hastily
43 "Gilligan's Island" homes
44 Hasty escape
45 Pager's sound
47 Put away (for)
51 Ahab's sighting
53 Popular topping
55 Corridors
56 Shirt brand name
57 "Do ___ others as . . ."
58 Kate's TV mate
59 Suffix with switch
60 No de Cologne?
61 Heston role
62 Called up
63 Matches a bet

DOWN
1 The F.B.I's J. ___ Hoover
2 "No man is an island" writer
3 Pass, as laws
4 Yale's home
5 Phillies park, familiarly
6 Film director Harold
7 Cleveland's lake
8 911 responders: Abbr.
9 Irrational speeches
10 Occupied, as a bathroom
11 Popular topping
12 Art Deco artist
13 Alejandro and Fernando
21 Say yes to
24 Ye ___ Book Shoppe
26 Jim Morrison's group, with "the"
27 Palmer's gallery
29 Ocho ___, Jamaica
30 Choice word
31 Muslim pilgrimage
32 Melville romance
33 Popular topping
34 Schmooze
37 Defeat, à la Ali
38 Base clearers
40 Gouda and Edam, e.g.
41 Top choice, so to speak
44 Pomeranian, for one
46 Miss ___ of "Dallas"
47 Dish's beloved, in rhyme
48 Gift recipient
49 Loosen the laces
50 Subatomic particles
51 Smack!
52 Angel's headgear
53 Berth place
54 Nehemiah preceder

by Stanley Newman

ACROSS

1 Assists
6 Group that votes alike
10 Tennis score
14 "So long, Simone"
15 Verdi opera
16 Local theater
17 Systematic, as instructions
19 Looks at
20 Faux ___
21 Stymie
23 Wampum
27 8/8/44
29 Old-fashioned curse word
30 Baseball's Espinoza
31 Writer Murdoch
32 Tiny bit
33 Tiniest sound
34 Blacktop basketball contest
37 Painful points
39 "Am ___ blame?"
40 1963 film "El ___"
43 Everything being taken into account
46 DCCLII doubled
47 60 secs.
49 Hebrew dry measure
50 Conceive
52 Unaffiliated politically: Abbr.
53 Nimble
54 Bryce ___ National Park
55 One of the Fates
57 Suffix with beat or peace
58 Move about
59 How a pendulum swings
66 Hot chamber

67 Lamb's pen name
68 Bathroom hanger
69 Hardly Mr. Cool
70 Bambi, e.g.
71 Ring-shaped island

DOWN

1 Is down with
2 N.Y.C. summer hrs.
3 Prevaricate
4 Energy
5 Poor, as a performance
6 Contralto's counterpart
7 On, as a lamp
8 Lyric poem
9 Abraham Lincoln, in a Whitman poem
10 Once more

11 Continually
12 Spain's peninsula
13 Fitted one within another
18 Rube
22 Green tea
23 Rand McNally products
24 Margarine
25 Repeatedly
26 Place for a pin
27 Food-related
28 Oversalivate
35 San Francisco player, for short
36 Roman name
38 Walk through puddles
41 Former Yugoslav chief
42 Tied
44 Laid on, as taxes
45 Permitted by law

47 One millionth of a meter
48 Smitten
51 Sioux Indian
56 Look after
57 Close
60 ___-de-France
61 Conk out
62 Drunkard
63 ___ Jima
64 Second smallest state: Abbr.
65 Right angle

by Wayne Robert Williams

47

ACROSS
1 Iraq's second-largest city
6 Drain problem
10 Actress Garr
14 Dominant
15 Hockey's Gordie
16 Flair
17 Poker loser's retort
20 Hindquarters
21 Western Indian
22 French fighter jet
23 Amo, ___, amat
24 Transfusion liquids
25 Ambiguity
30 Kind of loser
31 Publicizes
32 "How dry ___"
34 Plenty
35 Plaintiff or defendant
37 Cruel one
38 Midmorning
39 Slug
40 Twisted
41 Some baseball games
46 Bargain hunter's delight
47 Dental photo
48 Mummify
51 "King ___"
52 Apply with a light touch
55 Insurance provision
58 "___ just take a minute"
59 In ___ of
60 Golfer with an army
61 Prefix with gram or graph
62 Prevaricates
63 Gift ideas for prisoners?

DOWN
1 Foretoken
2 Ever and ___
3 Collar fastener
4 Morrow of "Quiz Show"
5 Savoir faire
6 Pick
7 Knowledge
8 Have
9 "There is no royal road to ___": Euclid
10 Ayatollah's capital
11 "On the Waterfront" director Kazan
12 Summoned, as a servant
13 "Picnic" playwright
18 Kin of etc.
19 Radials, e.g.
23 Fritzi Ritz, to Nancy
24 Show of anger
25 Distributed charity
26 Home of Maine's Black Bears
27 ___ Day (April 22)
28 Tony of cereal fame
29 Works hard for
30 Horror-film prop
33 Happened upon
35 Headlong
36 Toward shelter
37 Old-fashioned wedding word
39 "Hoops"
42 Of service
43 Uris bestseller
44 English composer Thomas
45 "Broadway Open House" regular, in 50's TV
48 Fix text
49 Speck of dust
50 Positive Wall Street figure
51 Banjo site, in song
52 Rackets
53 Eagerly expecting
54 Ciao, adiós etc.
56 Three, on a sundial
57 F.D.R.'s Blue Eagle grp.

by Jonathan Schmalzbach

48

ACROSS

1 "My Fair Lady" miss
6 ___ Air
9 Drop explosives on
13 Sal, in song
14 King topper
15 Kind of eclipse
16 Beethoven classic
19 Poker opener
20 Classic auto
21 Accountants' activities
22 Be under the weather
23 Electrical units
24 Horizontally
28 Leave the ground
29 Hint of scandal
30 "Gee whiz!"
31 Yearn (for)
35 Rarely
38 Jury member
39 Nobelist Wiesel
40 Adored
41 Mr. Musial
42 Evaluate
43 Adherents of Allah
47 Mine output
48 Gasoline rating
49 List ender
50 Native of old Peru
54 My sweetheart, in an old song
57 Core belief
58 Unknown John
59 Street urchin
60 Winged god
61 Neighbor of Syr.
62 Portents

DOWN

1 Austen heroine
2 City on the Rhône
3 "___ Rhythm"
4 Western novelist Grey
5 The whole shebang
6 Breakfast roll
7 Bounce back
8 Tennis call
9 German political groups
10 TV studio light
11 Lusterless finish
12 Copper-zinc alloy
15 Jeweler's eyeglass
17 Eye part
18 Chinese liquor
22 Spumante city
23 Bridal path?
24 Upon
25 Chaplin trademark
26 Houston school
27 Lollapalooza
28 Batman's partner
30 Swank affairs
31 Famous cookie man
32 Cabot ___ ("Murder, She Wrote" town)
33 Works the garden
34 Pass receivers
36 Tennis players
37 Otherwise
41 French legislature
42 St. Louis landmark
43 Grove of trees, in the Southwest
44 Yellow-orange
45 Dictation taker
46 Injures
47 Aquatic animal
49 Son in Genesis
50 Mideastern V.I.P.
51 Alaskan city
52 Originate, as a phrase
53 Miller and Sothern
55 Uganda's Amin
56 Sel

by Sidney L. Robbins

ACROSS

1 Church seat
4 Advantage
8 One way to enlarge a family
13 Essayist Wiesel
15 Projecting rock
16 "Casablanca" star, informally
17 Org.
18 Halloween imps
20 Retained
21 Jupiter's mother
22 Keanu of "Speed"
23 Map lines: Abbr.
25 Super joke
26 Listened
28 Cluckers
29 River of W.W. I
30 Vampire's tooth
31 Oxford, e.g.
35 Halloween visitors
38 Graf ___
39 Wedding shower?
40 French topper
41 Alternative to charge
42 Lüges
43 Freshen, in a way
46 Mimic
47 Place side by side
48 Evergreen
49 First of all
53 Halloween tale
55 Stare open-mouthed
56 Equestrian
57 City south of Moscow
58 Gaelic
59 Gland: Prefix
60 Small whirlpool
61 Court divider

DOWN

1 High spot
2 Otherwise
3 Tuft
4 Repeated
5 Throat-soothing candies
6 Chatters
7 Sunny-side-up item
8 Top nun
9 Measures (out)
10 Architectural arch
11 Moper
12 Hardy girl
14 Captivate
19 Juice source
24 Long journey
25 Style
26 Complain
27 Great Lake
28 Concoct
29 McKinley and others: Abbr.
30 Wiry rug fabric
31 Cheapest accommodations
32 Roundup group
33 Raw metals
34 N.Y. winter time
36 Declaims
37 Competent
41 Cuba's Fidel
42 With nimbleness
43 Garden insect
44 Lyric poem
45 1953 American League M.V.P. Al
46 Broadcast
47 Taj Mahal site
48 Tennessee Ernie ___
50 Mend
51 Church recess
52 Encounter
54 Stocking's end

by Sidney L. Robbins

ACROSS

1 ___ throat (winter ailment)
6 Duelists' steps
11 "20/20" network
14 Actress Dunne
15 Spartan magistrate
16 Interminable ride
19 Heavy reading
20 Mine yield
21 Parade stopper
22 Zenith
23 Each
24 Paragraph start
27 A.P. competitor
29 Where ships run aground
31 ___ Paulo
32 Grand site?
35 Speaker's stand
37 German article
38 "Sting like a bee" champion
39 Gum ball
41 Sony rival
42 Bit of butter
43 Castaway's call
44 Mighty mite
46 Portuguese money
48 Suffix with correspond
49 Client
51 Unit of radio frequency: Abbr.
52 Zone
55 "Savvy?"
57 Poet Pound
60 ___ Diamond
61 Diamonds, in slang
62 Applaud
63 Children's game
67 Kind of closet
68 Taco sauce
69 Understand
70 Amherst school, for short
71 More crafty

DOWN

1 Sis or bro
2 Scout unit
3 Parent, e.g.
4 Went in
5 Letterman's Stupid ___ Tricks
6 Nut for a nutcracker
7 Plant louse
8 Intricate problems
9 Long time
10 Matamoros Mrs.
11 Nick and Nora's pooch
12 Coalition
13 Mao's domain
17 Lachrymose
18 Aperture
25 Spring nymph
26 Lone Ranger's pal
28 Hawkeye State
30 Canal site
32 Gardner's stories
33 Single
34 "It's ___ way"
36 It's between Alta. and Man.
40 John ___ Passos
45 The M of "M.E."
47 One means of payment
50 With bounteousness
53 Shades
54 Unfolds
56 Gaggle members
58 Steak order
59 Church niche
63 Actor Gulager
64 Not her
65 Road curve
66 Mercury or Saturn

by Randall J. Hartman

ACROSS

1 Suspect's "out"
6 Start of an invention
10 ___ to riches
14 Chance
15 Potter's furnace
16 Taj Mahal site
17 "Slow down!"
19 Freshwater duck
20 Swapped
21 Villain's laugh
22 Peruvian native
23 Illiterates' signatures
25 Hammed it up
27 Army need
31 Got up again
34 Roebuck's partner
36 Aquarium fish
37 Charged atom
40 "Slow down!"
43 Antlered animal
44 Assessed
45 To incorrectly write an infinitive
46 Provide with feathers
48 Actress Harper
49 "Ridi, Pagliaccio" singer
53 Koch and others
55 Dublin's land
56 Defective missile
59 Hardened
64 X-ray vision blocker
65 "Slow down!"
67 Not punctual
68 Tire parts
69 Kind of ray
70 Glacial ridges
71 "No more!"
72 Wheat bundle

DOWN

1 Aid and ___
2 Tragic king
3 "___ boy!"
4 Hopalong Cassidy portrayer
5 The Dow, e.g.
6 50's voters "liked" him
7 TV signal receiver
8 Lamb pseudonym
9 Flower development
10 Proportion
11 Insurance worker
12 Princess of Monaco
13 Waldorf ___
18 German border river
24 Unruffled
26 Cat calls
27 Late tennis V.I.P.
28 Banquet
29 Lone Ranger attire
30 Table crumb
32 Cleared leaves
33 Jittery
35 Vassals
37 Capri, e.g.
38 Elevator pioneer
39 Earns as profit
41 Nose offenders
42 Likely
47 Cut-and-paste
49 String quartet member
50 Regions
51 Lariat
52 Beneath
54 Hosiery risks
57 Army outfit
58 Sample record
60 Mormons' home
61 Relative of hoarfrost
62 Poet Lazarus
63 Fall on ___ ears
66 Cobra

by Sidney L. Robbins

52

ACROSS
1 ___ Hatteras, N.C.
5 Clearheaded
10 Egyptian cobras
14 Mimics
15 Video arcade name
16 Turn obliquely
17 SCRAM
19 Antitoxins
20 Football's ___ Bowl
21 Safety org.
22 Current, as accounts
24 Russian grassland
26 Black Sea resort
28 Actors Silver and Howard
30 Illegal trader
33 Words preceding war or God
36 Young 'uns
38 Half of MCII
39 SPLIT
43 Indiana Jones's quest
44 Franchise
45 Vertical
46 Made tea
49 Crimson and carmine
51 Adulates
53 Standards of perfection
57 Plant pests
59 Italian wine district
61 Hawaiian garland
62 Cut in a skirt
63 BEAT IT
66 The Mikado's Lord High Executioner
67 Papal vestment
68 One of the Brontes
69 Suffix with road or hip
70 Opera voice
71 Miss Trueheart of the comics

DOWN
1 Summer getaways
2 "You'll always be ___ of me"
3 Tea type
4 Language ending
5 Yankee pitcher Don
6 Great Salt Lake state
7 Chocolate bean
8 Get on one's nerves
9 Allocate
10 St. Francis's home
11 VAMOOSE
12 Llama land
13 Barter
18 Finish
23 Dolt
25 Egg on
27 Mental confusion
29 Took deliberate steps
31 Grammy-winning Fitzgerald
32 Peril
33 Discoverers' cries
34 "Dead ___" (Dick Francis novel)
35 SKIDDOO
37 Hall-of-Famer Mel
40 Went too far
41 Finnan ___ (fish dish)
42 ___ dixit
47 Film cutter
48 Pea holder
50 One of two
52 Guy with a tail
54 "Home ___"
55 Shows partiality
56 Allies (with)
57 Proposes
58 Scheme
60 Normandy invasion town, 1944
64 Dander
65 Tell (on)

by Norman S. Wizer

ACROSS

1 Boats like Noah's
5 Dove, for one
10 Swiss mountain
13 "Star Wars" princess
14 Terre ___, Ind.
15 Bread with seeds
16 Huey Long roman à clef
19 Judith Krantz novel
20 It's frozen in Frankfurt
21 "For ___ a jolly . . ."
22 Secretary, e.g.: Abbr.
23 Canyon effect
25 Shoe bottom
29 Made as good as new
37 Marry
38 Eugene O'Neill work
42 Dye container
43 Most foulmouthed
44 Q-tip, e.g.
46 Bulletin board sticker
50 "Syncratic" prefix
54 Mauna ___
57 Letter before sigma
58 Streisand film, after "The"
61 Tale of a Piggy's plight
63 Lumberjack's tool
64 Loved ones
65 "Is so!" rebuttal
66 The ___ Affair
67 Gardner and others
68 Perches

DOWN

1 Visigoth leader
2 Hot dog topper
3 Potter's oven
4 Paige, informally
5 1988 Tim Rice musical
6 Squirrels' hangouts
7 Single-named novelist
8 Lab burners
9 Kathie Lee's co-host
10 Host
11 Soap ingredient
12 Stylus
17 With 39-Down, a cornball variety show
18 Speedy jets
19 Prominent part of "Peter Piper picked a peck . . ."
24 Refinery shipment
26 Possess
27 "Malcolm X" director
28 Magazine chiefs, for short
30 River to the North Sea
31 Health club
32 ___ Aviv
33 Scrap of food
34 Louis XIV, e.g.
35 Prior, to Prior
36 LP spinners
38 Boob tubes
39 See 17-Down
40 It's two after epsilon
41 Giant giant
45 Basketball's Larry
47 Passionate
48 Pieces of bedroom furniture
49 Feats of Clay: Abbr.
51 Radio part
52 Use logic
53 In base 8
54 Loamy soil
55 Incorrect
56 Brother of Prometheus
58 Clinton, slangily
59 Honor: Ger.
60 Four on a sundial
61 Loose
62 Petroleum company, informally

by Jonathan Schmalzbach

54

ACROSS

1 Winter precipitation
6 Pay, with "up"
10 Ivan the Terrible, e.g.
14 Proportion
15 "___ Smile" (1976 Hall & Oates hit)
16 Regulation
17 Bad loser's reaction
19 More than eager
20 Prolonged attack
21 Pacific Rim locale
23 "Eureka!"
24 ___ Vegas
26 A few
28 Scrutinizes
33 Watermelon's coat
34 "Tamerlane" playwright Nicholas
35 Frequent reduction targets
37 Delay
40 Outlawed explosion
42 Kind of service
43 Do ___ (all-out)
44 Take care of
45 Golf pegs
47 Author Ferber
48 Guided excursion
50 Innocent
52 Guy with a racket
55 Unknown John
56 Pleasant tune
57 Litigates
59 Train tracks
63 Ballet movement
65 Montana's state flower
68 Having little fat

69 Genesis son
70 ___ Rae (Sally Field role)
71 Flubs
72 Kind of tide
73 High-hat's look

DOWN

1 12th graders: Abbr.
2 Vientiane's land
3 Sewing case
4 It's west of England
5 Transverse pin
6 "___ matter of fact . . ."
7 California valley
8 Lock
9 Less difficult
10 ___-la-la
11 Gold digger's "mine"

12 Shalom in Hawaii
13 Like royalty
18 It's within grasp
22 Dispatch boat
25 Long-legged bird
27 Main dish
28 Nest eggs: Abbr.
29 Memo
30 Virginia women's college
31 Spaghetti sauces
32 Snooped
36 Race
38 Queue
39 Starring role
41 Race track tipsters
46 Gave an oath
49 Corned beef sandwich
51 Pines

52 Joplin's "___ Leaf Rag"
53 Ship from Kuwait
54 Marie Antoinette, e.g.
58 Greek portico
60 Remove the wrinkles from
61 Tradition
62 Not too many
64 Printers' measures
66 Recipe amt.
67 Old salt

by Sidney L. Robbins

ACROSS

1 Sobbed
5 Dangerous March date
9 First-class, in slang
14 Lotion ingredient
15 Kind of tide
16 Boisterous festivity
17 Bottle tops
18 ___ Rivera, Calif.
19 Warner ___ (Charlie Chan of film)
20 1943 musical composed by 37-Across
23 Poker opener
24 "High" time
25 Parts of table settings
28 Source of some PBS programs
29 Six-foot two, for example
33 Prying tool
34 Mother of Hermes
35 "Get outta here!"
36 Numero ___
37 Composer Kurt
38 Popular oil additive
39 Gabby bird
41 ___ of Fame
42 Grudge
44 Bridge option
45 Light switch positions
46 Loewe's partner on Broadway
47 Trudge
49 Othello's ancient
50 1928 work composed by 37-Across with "The"

57 Ache (for)
58 Moses' attire
59 One corner in Monopoly
60 Coke rival
61 Hardly ___ (rarely)
62 Sicilian's power
63 Vaudeville's Ole
64 June honorees
65 Sounds of reproof

DOWN

1 Texas city
2 Dash
3 John Paul, e.g.
4 Having a valid will
5 Feeds the computer
6 Clear the winter windshield
7 Apiece
8 One may be roseate
9 Utah city
10 Caves in
11 ___ the Terrible
12 Diner's card
13 Early auto maker
21 It's unique
22 Kind of point
25 Well-padded
26 See 31-Down
27 Three English rivers
28 Fights to save a sinking boat
30 Bret Harte character
31 With 26-Down, wife of 37-Across
32 Gentle runner
34 Rambled
37 Rodeo yell

40 Slander
42 Utah lily
43 Light plane
46 Cake features
48 Red Square figure
49 Not yet risen
50 Printer's goof
51 Dog command
52 Hip songs
53 Exploding star
54 Gobbles
55 Where to do figure eights
56 "Oh, woe!"

by Joy L. Wouk

56

ACROSS

1 Came up
6 Good farm soil
10 Son of Seth
14 1981 John Lennon hit
15 Formerly
16 Songbird
17 "Blithe Spirit" playwright
19 Wearing-out point for pants
20 Creek
21 Tidy
23 Vintage
24 Fr. ladies
26 Toboggans
28 Fondle
31 "Not guilty," e.g.
33 Stow in a ship's hold
36 ___ bomb
38 Miss Cinders of early comics
40 Spy work, for short
41 Songs sung from house to house
44 Succinct
45 Looped handle
46 Within: Prefix
47 Kind of hammer
49 Texas pioneer Houston et al.
51 ___ es Salaam
52 Midnights' counterparts
54 "Alice" diner
56 Pussy
58 Tie fabric
60 Lariats
64 Sills solo
66 Seasonal worker
68 Bridge feat
69 Heinz number, to Ovid?

70 Happening
71 "O ___ Night"
72 Town near Padua
73 Schmoes

DOWN

1 Bristles
2 Cheer (for)
3 Hebrew dry measure
4 City of witch hunts
5 Pitch tents
6 Temperature extreme
7 ___ even keel
8 Lots of lots
9 Military awards
10 Antlered animal
11 Not much time
12 Pitcher Hershiser
13 Calendar à la Variety

18 Eggs-and-cheese dish
22 Aquarium fish
25 1965 march site
27 Lawn mower brand
28 Agreements
29 Miss Barrymore
30 Like a downpour
32 Astronaut Shepard et al.
34 Upper ___ (now Burkina Faso)
35 TV newsman David
37 Err
39 State of India
42 Lilies
43 Minolta, e.g.
48 Isolate
50 Cut
53 Serbs and Croats

55 Round of cheers
56 Neither check nor charge
57 Singer Guthrie
59 Make stockings
61 Far East weight
62 Polly, to Tom
63 Fast planes
65 1948 song "Once in Love with ___"
67 Come out even

by Sidney L. Robbins

ACROSS

1 "Julius Caesar" role
5 Shall not, old style
10 Actress Drescher of "The Nanny"
14 The third man
15 Red, white or blue
16 San ___ (Riviera resort)
17 Uncle Ben's dish
18 Rod Stewart's ex
19 "What's ___ for me?"
20 James Cook ship
22 Hardy heroine
23 FedEx rival
24 Words after "Oh yeah?"
26 Smiles smugly
30 Doe's mate
32 "Tippy" boat
33 Henry Hudson ship
38 Tough-guy actor Ray
39 Corday's victim
40 Gen. Robt. ___
41 William Bradford ship
43 Sports facility
44 Charged particles
45 Shorebird
46 Indiana college
50 Coach Parseghian
51 A Great Lake
52 Sir Francis Drake ship
59 Breakfast order
60 Neeson and O'Flaherty
61 German-Polish border river
62 Avec's opposites

63 Stan's friend, in old films
64 Tableland
65 First word of Massachusetts's motto
66 Lawman Earp
67 "___ as 1, 2, 3"

DOWN

1 Mystery writer John Dickson ___
2 He had an Irish Rose
3 Private eyes, in slang
4 Butterine
5 Diving ducks
6 Romance novelist Victoria et al.
7 Jai ___
8 Taboo

9 Conduct, as business
10 Sen. Hollings
11 Extend, as a subscription
12 Some Mennonites
13 Untrue
21 One of the Gospels
25 Swelled head
26 Ripoff
27 ___ fides (bad faith): Lat.
28 ___ 500
29 Heliport site, often
30 Fillies' fathers
31 Moscow ruler
33 Sunup
34 ___ Beach, Fla.
35 Hgt.
36 Artist Magritte
37 Vintage

39 Clair de lune
42 Tell a whopper
43 A. A. Milne's first name
45 Coffee-maker switch
46 V-formation fliers
47 Sidewalk grinder's instrument
48 "Stop" and "Merge," e.g.
49 Novelist Hermann
50 Fess up
53 Unctuous
54 Carol syllables
55 "Fourth base"
56 Notion
57 An Untouchable
58 Cart

by Gregory E. Paul

58

ACROSS
1 Israeli port
6 "Of ___ I Sing"
10 Flattened circle
14 Fall flower
15 Is under the weather
16 Accumulation
17 It's lined with bars
19 Palindromic pop quartet
20 Irritate
21 Snoozing
23 "Just a ___"
26 Failures
27 Leadership group
32 Rigorous exams
34 Bay window
35 1985 film "___ Williams"
36 Mexican coin
40 Carte blanche
43 Fly alone
44 Identical
45 Identically
46 Rancher's cattle
47 Lawn pests
48 Ravel work
52 Lair
54 Polar covering
55 Makes watertight
61 When doubled, a Samoan port
62 1959 Doris Day film
66 Airline to Jerusalem
67 ___ Lackawanna Railway
68 Hawaiian island
69 Cowgirl Evans
70 Actor Alan
71 Won't

DOWN
1 Door holder
2 Late tennis V.I.P.
3 Followers: Suffix
4 Yard sections
5 Comic Johnson
6 Shape of St. Anthony's cross
7 That guy's
8 Yale Bulldog
9 Bake in sauce
10 October stones
11 Feelings, in slang
12 Playwright Edward
13 Bounds
18 "The A-Team" star
22 Stranded sailor's call
24 Central arteries
25 Indulged in reveries
27 Corny throwaways
28 Folkie Guthrie
29 Watch's face
30 Nevada city
31 Moose
33 Electrical unit
36 Game with sticks
37 Sinful
38 "For heaven's ___!"
39 Bullring cries
41 Impediment, at law
42 Computer capacity, for short
46 Mrs. in Madrid
48 Two-legged
49 Florida city
50 Over 21, liquorwise
51 Pierre's school
53 Sgt. or cpl.
56 Shoemaker's tools
57 Beehive state
58 Actress Turner
59 Part of K.K.K.
60 Comical playlet
63 Mr. Gershwin
64 Cover
65 Conducted

by Sidney L. Robbins

ACROSS

1 Movie spin-off TV series
5 "Arms and the Man" playwright
9 Little Goody Two ___
14 Director Preminger
15 Video
16 Blood vessel
17 With 37-Across and 59-Across, a familiar finale
19 With 58-Across, where to read 17-Across, etc.
20 Whooped
21 Combines
22 Appear
23 Sailor
24 Kind of ball
28 Naughty child's Christmas gift
32 Baden Baden, e.g.
35 English scarf
36 Israeli native
37 See 17-Across
40 Boxing site
41 "___ say more?"
42 Morse code message
43 Marsh growth
44 Much more expensive
45 Had been
46 Impressed deeply
50 Did a con job on
54 Mollified
58 See 19-Across
59 See 17-Across
60 Askew
61 French statesman Coty
62 Ripped
63 Rain gear
64 Bohemian
65 Raced

DOWN

1 Hole maker
2 One of the Three Musketeers
3 Inscribed pillar
4 According to ___
5 Agitate
6 "___ a nice day!"
7 Copied
8 Tie the knot
9 More secure
10 Kind of frost
11 Not secondhand: Abbr.
12 To be, in Paris
13 Pronounces
18 Logician's propositions
21 Hopping ___
23 Utmost extent
25 Fire residue
26 Play parts
27 Where Inchon is
28 Toy gun "ammo"
29 Sashes
30 Mr. Guthrie
31 Emulates hens
32 Twinkler
33 Skin opening
34 Author James
36 Meadowsweet
38 Pass receiver
39 Summer drink
44 "Dear old ___"
45 Bridge seats
47 Gentle breezes
48 Legally prevent
49 Moline, Ill., company
50 Penetrate
51 Pact since 1949
52 Mishmash
53 Whipping reminder
54 Insist
55 Confined, with "up"
56 Birds of ___
57 ___ Scott Decision, 1857
59 Pitcher's stat

by Sidney L. Robbins

60

ACROSS

1 Pizarro victim
5 ___ and dangerous
10 Rights org. estab. 1960
14 One who's socially challenged
15 With 4-Down, M.L.K. declaration of 8/28/63
16 Pentateuch: Var.
17 Gen. Bradley
18 Invoice word
19 "Love ___ leave it"
20 M.L.K. honor, 1964
23 In the past
24 Blaster's need
25 Passing mark
26 Cabinet department
31 Tosspot's spot
33 Chinese tea
34 Saint of Avila
36 Rights org. estab. 1942
38 Mr. Onassis
39 Rights org. led by M.L.K.
43 M.L.K. and others
47 Writer Rosten
48 ___ rasa
51 Inferential
54 Pizarro's theft from 1-Across
55 Up to, briefly
57 Luau dish
58 Song sung by M.L.K. and others
65 See 71-Across
66 Nonswimmer, maybe
67 Drawn tight
68 Hanging loosely
69 Surrounded by
70 Lawyer: Abbr.
71 With 65-Across, former French president
72 Play areas
73 Sci. class

DOWN

1 Aware of
2 Verne's captain
3 Cancer zodiacally
4 See 15-Across
5 Heathrow, e.g.
6 Onetime Korean president
7 Doll's cry
8 Force out
9 Peace policy
10 Swizzle
11 Handbill heading
12 M.L.K.'s alma mater, 1951
13 Drive recklessly
21 T-shirt size: Abbr.
22 Sch. orgs.
26 New Deal grp.
27 Cry of surprise
28 Bang up
29 Tête-à-tête
30 Ghostlike
32 ___ deferens
35 Marmalade ingredient
37 Outback bird
40 XV 3 X 11
41 Potok's "My Name is Asher ___"
42 Miler Sebastian
44 Lady Bird's middle name
45 One that keeps track?
46 Certain skiing events, slangily
48 Wrecker
49 Interstice
50 ___ University (where M.L.K. earned his doctorate)
52 Intersection: Abbr.
53 Candy mint
56 Andean animal
59 Ballyhoo
60 Scent
61 Sell
62 "Drat!" is a mild one
63 Silent
64 Word origin: Abbr.

by Walter Covell

ACROSS

1 This might be a lot
5 Paradigm
10 Sprite
13 Word after long or dog
14 Fragrance
15 Compete
16 Sydney of "The Maltese Falcon"
18 Lady of Eden
19 Added too many pounds
20 Displayed contempt
22 Snick's partner
23 Burglarize
26 Bummer
27 Lost Ark seekers?
30 Snatch
33 Where to hang one's hat
36 "Carmen" or "Aida"
37 Moline manufacturer
38 Alluring woman
40 Despondent
41 Upright
42 Goodnight lass
43 Steps over a fence
45 Hush-hush govt. org.
46 Gardener's item
47 ___ Palace
49 Cape Canaveral org.
51 Hardly bold
52 Sandy's barks
56 Interviewer Barbara
59 Restaurant
61 Levin who wrote "Deathtrap"
62 "Of Thee I Sing" role
65 Kind of horn
66 It's enough to bring a tear to the eye
67 Swiftness
68 Owned
69 Neck parts
70 Steps on the evolutionary ladder

DOWN

1 Baseball's Hank
2 Minotaur's home
3 Short jacket
4 Poet Millay
5 Welcome giver?
6 Bruin Bobby
7 Accomplishes
8 Corrects
9 Afterward
10 Landscaping item
11 As we speak
12 Oats, e.g.
13 Urges, with "on"
17 Undress
21 Anxious
24 Texas city
25 Scolds
28 Top-notch
29 Red vegetable
31 Firecracker paths
32 Obsolescent VCR format
33 Letters before omegas
34 Cork's site
35 It was colonized circa A.D. 986
37 Fawn or doe
39 "This foolishness must ___ once!"
44 Kind of cake
47 Canopus's constellation
48 Minor despot
50 Affix, as a button
53 Della of pop
54 Stews
55 "Auld Lang ___"
56 Accompanying
57 Coloratura's piece
58 Cut
60 Turkish honcho
63 Shoe part
64 Printers' measures

by Sidney L. Robbins

62

ACROSS

1 Person with a beat
4 Mafia kingpin
8 Keeps one's fingers crossed
13 Voiced
15 Prime draft status
16 Maine college town
17 Deal with quickly
20 Isolate, in a way
21 I.O.U.
22 Phila. clock setting
23 N.F.L. linemen: Abbr.
24 Prince Valiant's firstborn
26 ___ Moines
28 Save steps
35 Point one's finger at
37 Panorama
38 Too
39 Prefix with type
40 Actress Thompson et al.
41 Traveling type
42 Mideast chief
43 "Gypsys, Tramps & Thieves" singer
44 Politico Jackson
45 Is easily riled
48 China's Chou En-___
49 Yang's partner
50 Ancient text "___ Te Ching"
53 They give you a shot in the arm
56 Pre-1917 honcho
59 Guitar feature
61 Be cheated
64 Speechify
65 "Pretty Woman" star
66 "Alas"
67 Morocco's capital
68 Medical suffix
69 Elephant's weight, maybe

DOWN

1 Promising rookie
2 Long-armed ape, informally
3 Islamabad denizens
4 Hold fast
5 Enero to diciembre
6 Fringe benefit, for short: Var.
7 ___ of office
8 Owl
9 Hockey's Bobby
10 Jab
11 Country Slaughter
12 Squeezable
14 "___ Misérables"
18 Allay, as thirst
19 Word before peak or walk
25 Indian rug
27 Wells Fargo vehicles
29 Unconcerned with right and wrong
30 East ___ (Manhattan resident)
31 Substantial, as a meal
32 Seal
33 Exploits
34 Ripped
35 Insipid
36 Peru's capital
40 Unstable person, slangily
44 Coup d'état group
46 Perfumed bag
47 Angles
51 Prefix with meter
52 Versifier Nash
53 Mr. Sikorsky
54 Actress Miles
55 Knife
57 Golden Fleece ship
58 Atlas lines: Abbr.
60 Genetic stuff
62 Amtrak term.
63 Dernier ___

by Ernie Furtado

ACROSS
1 Office note
5 Buss
10 Fiddler, for one
14 Gung-ho
15 It's grasping
16 Catcher's base
17 Margaret Rutherford film portrayal
19 Skin cream ingredient
20 Peculiar
21 Goddess of discord
22 Apprehend
24 Part of R.O.T.C.
26 1963 Pulitzer biographer Leon
27 Gettysburg general
28 1984 Tom Selleck film
32 Author __ Chandler Harris
35 Tartan wearer
37 Succinctly worded
38 Worrier's woe, they say
40 Weed digger
41 Vista
42 Tiny: Prefix
43 Poet Sexton
45 Canine command
46 Utah banned in 1882
48 Doctors' org.
50 Wisecrack
51 Lobbed explosive
55 Polemist
58 Humanities
59 Checkers side
60 Auto racer Yarborough
61 Mickey Spillane film portrayal

64 Quiz choice
65 "The Tempest" sprite
66 "Earth in the Balance" author
67 Detected
68 Mary Poppins, e.g.
69 Hoarse horse?

DOWN
1 Thatcher's successor
2 Dodge
3 In one's __ eye
4 Pindar product
5 Goes on a crash diet
6 One of the Osmonds
7 Heidi's home
8 Newspaper feature: Abbr.

9 Prepares dough
10 Warner Oland film portrayal
11 Part to play
12 Andy's pal on old radio
13 Sugar source
18 Only
23 Takes five
25 Ralph Bellamy film portrayal
26 Chowed down
28 Bonkers
29 Nest site
30 Anglo-Saxon worker
31 Lively dance
32 Start, as a dead battery
33 Mishmash
34 Book after Proverbs: Abbr.
36 __ at the bit

39 Scalawag
44 Temporal
47 Eddie Rickenbacker, e.g.
49 Arizona city
51 Environmentally-minded
52 Knight's suit
53 Plow man
54 King Edmund's successor
55 "Hamlet" has five of them
56 Pink, as steak
57 Borden product
58 Analogous
62 Kin of a Keogh plan: Abbr.
63 Selznick studio

by Gregory E. Paul

64

ACROSS

1. ___ Park, N.Y.
5. Cider season
9. Layer of paint
13. Kind of collar
14. Together, musically
15. 1982 Stallone action role
16. Florsheim product
17. With 62-Across, words of caution
19. Sen. Kennedy
20. Mr. Lugosi
21. Athletes' negotiators
22. Spartacus, e.g.
24. Wing: Prefix
26. Intelligent sea creature
28. Early American statesman ___ King
33. Vituperate
35. How some packages are sent
37. Small rail bird
38. Ones who don't enunciate
40. Lashes down
42. City near Monaco
43. Restaurant bill
45. Tropical eels
46. Scouts do good ones
48. Diet
50. Australian marsupial
52. Muse of poetry
55. Catered event
59. Lawyers' degrees
61. Auto part
62. See 17-Across
64. "___ boy!"
65. Sea eagles

66. Actor James ___ Jones
67. "Portnoy's Complaint" author
68. 6-3, 4-6, 6-1, e.g.
69. "___ bien!" (French accolade)
70. Carpet layer's calculation

DOWN

1. Pauses
2. Singer Waters
3. With 30-Down, what 17- and 62-Across are
4. A quarter of four
5. Lose color
6. Newspaper publisher Ochs
7. Asylum resident
8. Permit
9. Neanderthals' home
10. Harbinger
11. Adjoin
12. Take these out for a spin
15. Harshness
18. Civil War vets' org.
20. ___ of the ball
23. Canceled
25. Biblical son
27. Sprightly
29. Underworld money lender
30. See 3-Down
31. Chemistry Nobelist Harold
32. Lip
33. Sunder
34. Writer Wiesel

36. Moore of "Indecent Proposal"
39. F.D.R.'s mother, ___ Delano
41. Arrives
44. Protective glass cover
47. On the ___ (declining)
49. In abundance
51. ___ pro nobis
53. Sip
54. D-Day beach
55. Thumbs-up votes
56. Golfer's shout
57. Allen of "Candid Camera"
58. War deity
60. Oil quantities: Abbr.
63. Still and all
64. Mr. Gershwin

by Sidney L. Robbins

ACROSS
1 March instrument
5 Succeed in life
10 Brigham Young's home
14 Desertlike
15 Sky blue
16 Jesus' attire
17 Date tree
18 Sight at sunup
20 "___ Need Is the Girl" ("Gypsy" song)
21 Nav. rank
22 Hosts' counterparts
23 Nullify
25 Has ___ with
26 Undamaged
28 Hemmed
32 Move like a crab
33 Membership on Wall Street
34 Days of the dinosaurs
35 Card game
36 Salesmen sometimes leave them
39 Neighbor of Md.
40 Touch
42 N.B.A. star Thurmond
43 Escorted
45 Capital of Baja California Norte
47 Early invaders of England
48 Gallup product
49 Father, to Li'l Abner
50 International org.
53 Untold centuries
54 Butterfingers's cry
57 Stamp on some mail
59 Tallow source
60 Baldie's head
61 Individual items
62 Narrowly defeat
63 Jim-dandy
64 Discharge
65 Destine for trouble

DOWN
1 Tidbit in Toledo
2 Caspian feeder
3 Love letter
4 Halsey, for one
5 Most willing
6 Layer in the atmosphere
7 Minks and sables
8 Prince Valiant's firstborn
9 Flare up again
10 Imperativeness
11 Bushy clumps
12 Help in the holdup
13 Chops
19 Night in Nimes
24 Court coups
25 Start of a Dickens title
26 Farrakhan's belief
27 Weeper of myth
28 Seven: Prefix
29 "Hello"
30 Watergate Senator Sam
31 College heads
33 Minute
37 Similar item
38 Light punishment
41 Race track figure
44 Told all about
46 Caesar's partner in 50's TV
47 Most reasonable
49 Displays petulance
50 Sweeping hairstyle
51 Lunchtime
52 Salinger girl
53 Actress Adams
55 "___ My Heart" (1913 hit)
56 Stalk
58 Chang's Siamese twin

by Bernice Gordon

66

ACROSS
1 Mosquito marks
6 It might be arched
10 Talks gangsta-style
14 "The Tempest" spirit
15 Country path
16 Dutch cheese
17 Pirates' flag
19 Medical researcher's goal
20 Aardvark snacks
21 More than big
22 Onetime hostess Maxwell
23 ___ Alamos
24 Spendthrift
26 Goods cast overboard
30 Halts
32 Kind of label
33 Con artist's aide
34 Baden-Baden, e.g.
37 Popular sort
40 Take advantage of
41 Unaccompanied
42 Clamor
43 Babble
44 In the open, as beliefs
45 High-spirited horses
48 Etch A Sketch, e.g.
49 Mil. defense systems
50 Escargot
53 Book after Job
57 Swag
58 All-for-one feeling
60 It's just for openers

61 Russia's Mountains
62 Make amends
63 Antler wearer
64 Red-ink amount
65 Stared open-mouthed

DOWN
1 ___ California
2 Collar straightener
3 Pinball no-no
4 Slippery fish
5 On the ___ (furtively)
6 Lumps
7 Fury
8 Change for a five
9 "___ of London" (1935 film)
10 Playtime
11 Grown-up
12 Analyze grammatically
13 Libel
18 Kitchen, e.g.
23 Rigging rope
25 In generous amounts
26 Amulet
27 Son of Seth
28 Bathroom feature
29 The sun
30 Glowed
31 Cause of beach erosion
33 Lampblack
34 Use a letter opener
35 Sit
36 Overwhelmed
38 Generous drink serving

39 Mauna ___
43 Ask, ask, ask
44 Like Lindbergh's flight
45 Meal starter
46 Hearty steak
47 Overact
48 Money drawers
51 Roman "fiddler"
52 "Oh, woe!"
53 Movie pooch
54 Mince
55 Fork prong
56 Hightailed it
59 Joker

by Sidney L. Robbins

ACROSS

1 City near Kyoto
6 Saturate
10 Gallows reprieve
14 Threesome
15 "So long"
16 Cro-Magnon's home
17 Jungle dweller
20 Poet and tentmaker's son
21 It's unique
22 Buckeye State
25 Burn
27 Christopher of "Superman"
31 Campaigned
32 Sunday songs
34 Anticrime boss
35 Zest
38 Synthetic rubber
40 17-Across's formal title
43 Ailments
44 Skirt movement
46 Elderly
47 Descendant
50 Opposite WNW
51 Bowling lane button
53 Playwright David
54 Like target pigeons
55 Pout
57 Mrs. Peel from "The Avengers"
59 Phrase from 17-Across
66 Declare
67 Legal memo starter
68 Kind of eclipse
69 Sneaky look
70 Constellation component
71 Stage direction

DOWN

1 Giant slugger
2 Mexican Mrs.
3 Inner-tube innards
4 Hummer's instrument
5 Edenite
6 Building floor, in London
7 Lummox
8 Johnnie Cochran, e.g.
9 Actress Madeline
10 Ray Bolger film role
11 Astaire specialty
12 "Hail, Caesar!"
13 "___, ma'am"
18 Partner of Crosby and Stills
19 Always, to a poet
22 Assn.
23 Trucker's business
24 Shoe pads
26 More than forgetfulness
28 Old Testament prophet
29 Singer Williams
30 Before
33 Message from the Titanic
36 NBC's peacock, e.g.
37 Uneven
39 Two of these make a qt.
41 Platoon members, for short
42 Coward
43 Deface
45 Relative of "pssst!"
48 Complier
49 Jules Verne captain
52 Craggy peak
54 Kind of cooking
56 Terrorists' weapons
58 Wagon train puller
59 Glove compartment item
60 Mate of 5-down
61 Golf ball's perch
62 Gun lobby grp.
63 Colony pest
64 Scot's denial
65 Flub

by Randall J. Hartman

68

ACROSS
1 Writer Tom or Thomas
6 Help in crime
10 One ___ (form of baseball)
14 Of the lower intestine
15 Ready for picking
16 Canceled, as a launch
17 Neato
19 One more time
20 Glimpses
21 ___ do well
23 Referee's count
24 Household power: Abbr.
26 Phoenix neighbor
28 ___ been
31 Cuticle shaper
36 Patriot Allen
38 "Crazy" bird
39 Hydroxyl compound
40 Eins + zwei
41 Court center, usually
42 Hawaii's state bird
43 Loses all power
44 Did better than a B
45 Welsh dog
46 Curry favor with
49 ___ Diego
50 Golfer Ballosteros
51 List ender
53 ___ jongg
55 "Masque of Alfred" composer
58 Eats away, as soil
62 ". . . ___ saw Elba"
64 Kid's bike part
66 Polaris, e.g.
67 Scent
68 Crowded
69 Fictional Mr.
70 Exhibit boredom
71 Mr. Kefauver

DOWN
1 Towel (off)
2 Corrida cheers
3 Jump
4 Prima ___ evidence
5 Level of command
6 Couples' transportation?
7 Good: Fr.
8 Fencer's blade
9 Urban housing
10 End ___ high note
11 Receptacles
12 "A Death in the Family" writer James
13 Burg
18 River through Flanders
22 Legal matter
25 Printed cloth
27 Shorthand taker
28 Gossipy Hopper
29 In position, as a sail
30 ___ Bay, Brooklyn
32 Unusual
33 Sweet treat
34 Afro Cuban drum
35 Anne of fashion
37 Usher's route
41 Fledgling entrepreneur
45 Message in mime
47 ___ Marie Saint
48 Anna who played Nana
52 Comes in last
53 Netting
54 Pretentious
56 It means nothing to Julio
57 Plenty, old-style
59 Fender bender memento
60 Ill at ___
61 Fr. holy women
63 Dander
65 Prince Valiant's son

by Ernie Furtado

ACROSS

1 "You can say that again"
6 Papa's partner
10 Plays on stage
14 Perfection
15 Son of Adam
16 Tropical root
17 Tuxedo, slangily
19 Collar type
20 Otherwise
21 Starry
23 Computer headache
24 Nursery rhyme Jack
26 Counters by argument
28 Jam bottle
31 Push
32 Prophet
33 "___ Yankee Doodle dandy"
34 Like most colleges today
35 Taj Mahal site
38 Book before James
40 Inventory
43 "I Do, I Do, I Do, I Do, I Do" singers
44 With 22-Down, a cake brand
45 Imitate
46 Bumstead dog and namesakes
49 Cut, as nails
50 Visibly embarrassed
51 This and ___
52 Horseshoers' tools
54 "The Raven" poet
56 "Not a ___ too soon"
58 Pete Sampras org.

62 Novelist Paton
64 Locomotive's front
66 Become fatigued
67 Leg's middle
68 Don't exist
69 Jay Leno, e.g.
70 Three feet
71 Absorbs books

DOWN

1 Two nickels
2 Object of adoration
3 7 1 3, 5 1 5, 1 1 9, etc.
4 Instances of filming
5 Bullring shout
6 Rubdowns
7 Adjoined
8 Israel's Golda
9 Priests' places
10 Feasted
11 Second-story man
12 Rainbow fish
13 Hymnal contents
18 Peter of Peter, Paul & Mary
22 See 44-Across
25 Purplish brown
27 Schnozzola
28 Holy war
29 One-celled animal
30 V on a TV?
36 Lariat
37 Matured
39 Impetuous
40 On an even keel
41 Beard of grain
42 Li'l Abner's creator
44 Carpenter, often
47 Sweet potato

48 Solid and sturdy
53 Capital of Bolivia
54 Lane
55 Mixture
57 ___ Lisa
59 Mets milieu
60 Take care of
61 Partner of crafts
63 Basketball champion's "trophy"
65 Old salt

by Sidney L. Robbins

ACROSS

1 Mineral powder
5 Country singer Buck
10 ___ Clayton Powell
14 Sills solo
15 Hypothesize
16 "___ la Douce"
17 Musical based on "The Taming of the Shrew"
19 Garden starter
20 Book after Nehemiah
21 "Oh, to be in ___": Browning
23 Infuriated
26 City near Provo
27 Mrs. Mertz
30 Parapsychology skill
32 "Wuthering Heights" man
35 ___ Rabbit
36 Wish for
38 Give ___ whirl
39 Cartoonist Keane
40 Musical based on "The Once and Future King"
41 Diamond stat
42 Wriggler
43 Without secrets
44 Keogh, for one
45 Waggish
47 Initials on a record label
48 "Play ___ for Me"
49 Bucks and does
51 Slip-up
53 Double ___ (rat)
56 Worry free place
60 Scream
61 Musical based on "7½ Cents" with "The"
64 Sandwich shop
65 Poetry Muse
66 Suffix with cell or gland
67 Cowboy Rogers's real last name
68 Politician ___ Alexander
69 Adm. Zumwalt

DOWN

1 Seize
2 Onassis and others
3 Roster
4 One who works the till
5 "Fidelio," e.g.
6 Chinese cooker
7 That: Sp.
8 Day's opposite, in commercials
9 Court reporter
10 Having walkways
11 Musical based on the Supremes
12 Prayer ending
13 Hwy. Safety org.
18 Blackbird
22 Welcome
24 One that swarms
25 Central nature
27 Receded
28 City on the Mosel
29 Musical based on "The Matchmaker"
31 Parthenon feature
33 Up, in baseball
34 Save for a ___ day
36 Dangle bait on the water
37 Artist Lichtenstein
40 Nat and Natalie
44 Indian dugout
46 Singer Uggams
48 Manny of the Dodgers
50 Drive back
52 Scuttlebutt
53 Dancer Charisse et al.
54 Lively dance
55 ___ avis
57 Gloomy shadow
58 Muslim leader
59 Flying: Prefix
62 Toast topper
63 One ___ time

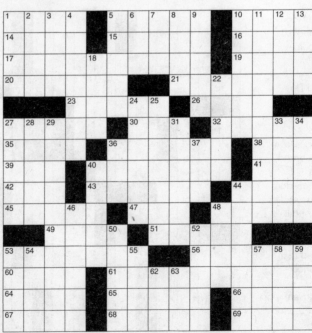

by Gregory E. Paul

ACROSS

1 The two together
5 "Woman __ Year"
10 Egg layer
13 Distant
15 Nevada lake resort
16 King Kong, e.g.
17 TV oldie
20 Up-to-date
21 Boston's __ nickname, with "the"
22 Require
23 Buffalo locale
25 Charged particle
27 Blue
30 Prevaricator
31 Alternatives to tricks
35 Dined
36 Suffix with beat or refuse
37 Verboten
38 TV oldie
43 "I do" location
44 Possess
45 4:00 gathering
46 Gawks
48 Tail movements
50 Double curve
51 Dictator Amin
52 Hitchcock's "The 39 __"
54 It might be a convertible
57 Flood's opposite
59 Comfort
63 TV oldie
66 Be bedbound
67 Expunge
68 Plants with fronds
69 Caught
70 Lusterless finish
71 Glut

DOWN

1 Healing lotion
2 Bread spread
3 Horned __ (lizard)
4 Move like a helicopter
5 Giant Mel
6 TV oldie
7 Grand amount
8 Middle Earth inhabitant
9 Extra wide shoe size
10 Possess
11 Sporting blade
12 Uncool fellow
14 Savage
18 Diamond division
19 Temper, as glass
24 Earth goddess: Var.
26 Morsels
27 Drawn-out tales
28 Inclined
29 T.W.A. rival
32 Lessen
33 Musical sounds
34 Ice cream drinks
39 Cowboy's rope
40 Angered
41 Police __ team
42 Swallow
47 __ Club (conservationists' group)
49 Lampoon
53 Blackthorn shrubs
54 Beau for a doe
55 Buckeye State
56 Pool table cover
58 Finish ahead of
60 Taj Mahal site
61 Not worth a red __
62 Latin being
64 Skirt edge
65 Discern

by Randall J. Hartman

72

ACROSS

1 Extremely unpleasant
6 One going downhill
10 Sand
14 Cosmetician Lauder
15 Peel
16 ___ Rooter
17 With 36-Across, shirker's comment
20 Manipulates a needle
21 60 minutes past 12
22 Thrusts back
23 ___ Glory
24 Glad rags
25 Changed into
29 English statesman William
30 Oak-to-be
31 ___ California
32 Land amount
36 See 17-Across
39 Lays turf
40 Biddies
41 Siouan Indian
42 Poses
43 Made beer
44 Inclines
47 Serling of "The Twilight Zone"
48 Actor Omar
49 Artfully shy
50 Gem
54 Evasion and pursuit
57 Came to earth
58 Leave out
59 British Museum's ___ marbles
60 The "B" in N.B.
61 Dig this!
62 Yorkshire city

DOWN

1 Front-page matter
2 Tennis V.I.P. Arthur
3 Goulash
4 Counting system
5 Still and all
6 Disburse
7 Spike, as the punch
8 Time for the history books
9 Of waste
10 Pick of the vineyard
11 Oarsman
12 Country in a grand tour
13 Santa's bagful
18 Bagel's middle
19 Mailed
23 Hotel chain name

24 South Pacific islanders
25 Faces the pitcher
26 Reverberate
27 Campus lass, in old lingo
28 Weaponry
29 Dupes
31 Borscht ingredients
32 Cathedral area
33 Eagle feature
34 Latest "in" fashion
35 Observed critically
37 Leader's office
38 The Almighty
42 Twirl
43 Word before and after "will be"
44 Laminated rock

45 Former language of 12-Down
46 Give a keynote address
47 Course
48 Sign of healing
49 Mint
50 Leer at
51 Senate runner
52 In the center of
53 Camera part
55 2,001 to Ovid
56 Slippery fish

by Sidney L. Robbins

ACROSS

1 Ties one's shoes
6 Wise one
10 Haberdasher's wares
14 Full-price payer, at an amusement park
15 Female egg
16 Jai ___
17 Casals's instrument
18 Handful of hay
19 1994 Jodie Foster movie
20 Arranged unfairly
23 Caboodle's partner
24 Hearty draught
25 Demanded proof
34 Mountain nymph
35 "___ From Muskogee" (1970 hit)
36 The sun
37 Bundle up
38 Cloak-and-dagger types
40 Positive
41 ___ Alamos
42 Crimson rivals
43 Suit material
44 Upped the stakes
48 Actress Sue ___ Langdon
49 ___ de Cologne
50 Remained expressionless
58 Singer Brickell
59 Where Anna taught
60 Parade component
62 Type of group
63 ___ of Man
64 Stage in a butterfly's development
65 ___ 500
66 Require
67 All over

DOWN

1 Varnish ingredient
2 Summer refreshers
3 Unorthodox sect
4 Fitzgerald of scat
5 Supplied
6 Site of a 1976 South African uprising
7 Gung-ho
8 Sudden wind
9 Stress
10 "Messiah" composer
11 Sheltered
12 Bath powder
13 Imported material
21 Tease
22 North Sea tributary
25 Monks' hoods
26 Traffic directional
27 Alternative to purchase
28 In the ___ of luxury
29 Hubbub
30 ___ out (supplement)
31 Seize without authority
32 Relinquish
33 Armada
38 Ignores the alarm
39 Wrestling finale
40 Understand
42 Sicilian spouter
43 Mix up kings and queens?
45 Diner
46 Considered
47 Paver's need
50 French military cap
51 Shangri-La
52 ___ Piper
53 River to the Seine
54 Hardy cabbage
55 Broadway's ___ Jay Lerner
56 Electricity carrier
57 Roof overhang
61 Little bit

by Kenneth Witte

ACROSS

1 I.B.M. rival
6 How a deer might attend a party?
10 Info
14 Unobstructed
15 Peru's capital
16 Historic periods
17 Seaside aerialist
19 Give orders
20 Pass receivers
21 Repair
22 Movie pooch
23 Mata Hari, e.g.
24 Hold in high regard
26 Morality
30 Judge Ito
32 Miss Morgenstern of 70's TV
33 "If You Knew ___, Like . . ." (1925 hit)
34 Ft. Worth campus
37 Unburden oneself
40 German spa
41 "Yours ___" (letter closing)
42 Two under par
43 Smiles broadly
44 Lovers' meetings
45 B flat equivalent
48 Wall Street order
49 Booty
50 Starman
53 Birthday party necessity
57 Not keep a secret
58 Loiter
60 Architect Saarinen
61 Without repetition
62 Mr. Burr
63 Water whirl
64 Card game for three
65 Rio de la ___

DOWN

1 Yearn
2 Blueprint
3 Remain unsettled
4 Stays behind
5 Energy unit
6 Like algae
7 Ebb, e.g.
8 "You said it, brother!"
9 Corsage flower
10 Pre-election event
11 Came up
12 Discernment
13 Silkmaking region
18 Baby holders
23 Strew about
25 Stage background
26 Gardner of mysteries
27 Those characters
28 Romantic attraction, slangily
29 Uganda's Amin
30 Soothes
31 Wan
33 Rundown area
34 Clothes
35 Close-knit religious group
36 Salt Lake City athletes
38 Algonquian group
39 Jovial
43 Diamond helper
44 ___ fish sandwich
45 "Virginia Woolf" playwright
46 Like shoes
47 Squirrel away
48 Sire, biblically
51 Tall and thin
52 Early Peruvian
53 Newcastle's pride
54 Atmosphere
55 Shoelace problem
56 Author Ferber
59 Some MTV music

by Sidney L. Robbins

ACROSS

1 Out on ___ (vulnerable)
6 Jefferson's predecessor
11 Bleat
14 Novelist Puzo
15 Craze
16 Elbow's locale
17 With 37- and 64-Across, a seasonal observation
19 Here, in Paris
20 Secondhand transaction
21 Summer in Le Havre
22 Thin nail
23 Red vegetable
25 Scales, as a ladder
27 Sheltered, nautically
30 Cribbage marker
32 It's a plus
33 "Coriolanus" costume
34 Antenna
37 See 17-Across
43 Agreeable responses
44 Corncob or briar, e.g.
45 Shopping run
49 Health club
50 Strategize
51 ___ house (carnival attraction)
54 Star-Kist product
56 Dry
57 Greek letters
59 Easter floral display
63 Newsman Rather
64 See 17-Across
66 Pindar's pride

67 Mystery writers' award
68 Poet Stephen Vincent ___
69 Commit matrimony
70 Oceans
71 Heavenly spots

DOWN

1 From the U.S. Abbr.
2 Wash
3 Angers
4 French Revolutionary statesman
5 Actor Peter of "Taxi Driver"
6 Electrical unit, informally
7 Venture
8 Author Loos

9 "Back to the salt ___"
10 Droop
11 Scottish kids
12 Roofed in gallery
13 In the center of
18 Cause of unwanted moisture
22 Egyptian god of music
24 Overflows (with)
26 Baby bovine
27 One ___ time
28 Actress Myrna
29 Sense of self
31 Lawn greenery
35 All thumbs
36 Battery's partner
38 Reply to a refusenik
39 Horrified
40 Zero

41 Tax figurer, for short
42 Urge
45 Figure at one's side
46 Macy's event
47 Destroyed
48 Terminus
52 Ooze
53 Mournful tune
55 Weeper of myth
58 Rice Krispies sound
60 "The Last Days of Pompeii" girl
61 On the level
62 Rigidifies
64 Koppel or Kennedy
65 Grads-to-be

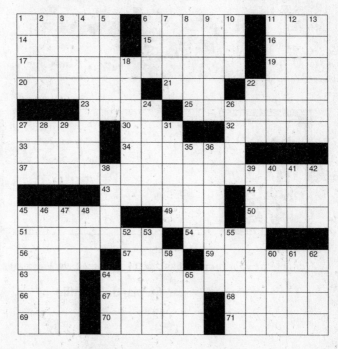

by Sidney L. Robbins

The New York Times

Crossword Puzzle Collections

THE BOOKS THAT ARE ON EVERYBODY'S WISH LIST!

Available at your local bookstore or online at www.nytimes.com/nytstore

St. Martin's Griffin

1

```
B O A R D ■ D E F T ■ I D E A
A G R E E ■ E L I A ■ M E S H
G E T S T O F I R S T B A S E
S E E ■ A R I ■ S T A R D O M
■ ■ M I E N ■ E C U ■ ■ ■
O U T I N L E F T F I E L D
T S A R S ■ R O U T ■ O V A
T I M E ■ S T O O L ■ A C I D
O N E ■ S I D S ■ A M A N A
■ G R A N D S T A N D P L A Y
■ ■ F O E ■ L A D S ■ ■
D I A G R A M ■ P S I ■ M A O
I N T H E R E P I T C H I N G
E T N A ■ M E A N ■ T U D O R
M O O N ■ S K Y E ■ S E I N E
```

2

```
B A J A ■ R A T A ■ S T A K E
I D O L ■ E W E R ■ T E S L A
D E L L ■ W A R T ■ E N T E R
E L L ■ G A Y N I N E T I E S
T A Y L O R ■ ■ S A L E ■ ■
■ ■ R E A D E R ■ G E R M A N
G H O S T ■ T A M E R ■ E R E
R A G E ■ M O T E L ■ K R I S
I V E ■ H A N E S ■ A I R E S
T E R R O R ■ D A I N T Y ■
■ ■ E L A M ■ S T E W E D
H A P P Y T R A I L S ■ I D A
A T E A M ■ M O R A ■ A D I N
M A R I A ■ O N A N ■ B O N D
S T E R N ■ M E N D ■ S W A Y
```

3

```
E C H O ■ Y O G A ■ H U M I D
C L O D ■ E V E N ■ U T I C A
L A R D ■ M E T S ■ D A R E D
A S S ■ J E R S E Y S H O R E
T H E C A N ■ ■ L E O ■ ■
■ R O P I N G ■ A N S W E R
O M A H A ■ A L A R ■ T H R U
P O C O N O M O U N T A I N S
A V E R ■ N E W T ■ R I T E S
L E S T W E ■ S O F I N E
■ ■ R A E ■ U P S H O T
T H E H A M P T O N S ■ O W E
A U R I C ■ C O R N ■ L U N D
F L I C K ■ O N C E ■ U S E D
T A N K S ■ T E A L ■ V E R Y
```

4

```
L A D D ■ R I V E R ■ C H E R
A W A Y ■ E M I L E ■ L I V E
M A N E E V E N T S ■ A R I A
A R E ■ L I T ■ O I L W E L L
S E S A M E ■ A N N I E ■ ■
■ ■ I O W A N ■ S E D A T E
W E A R ■ E X E S ■ S M I R K
A L D A ■ D E M O S ■ O D I E
F L A P S ■ S O F T ■ N A P S
T E M P U S ■ N A I V E ■
■ A M P L E ■ N I T W I T
S C O R P I O ■ A K A ■ O R E
L O V E ■ C R E W E L H O A X
O M E N ■ E N T E R ■ B E T A
B E R T ■ S E E D S ■ O D E S
```

5

```
O V E R ■ M A C E D ■ D U S T
P E L E ■ E N L A I ■ O T O E
T R A F A L G A R S Q U A R E
S O L E N O I D ■ A U G H T S
■ ■ R O D E ■ B L A H ■
R E M E D Y ■ C O L D ■ A G A
I V A N A ■ S O L O ■ I L E S
C I R C L E T H E W A G O N S
E T R E ■ N A N S ■ S N O R E
R A Y ■ E G I S ■ S T O K E S
■ ■ Y S E R ■ F E H R ■
A N D E A N ■ A I R M A I L S
B E R M U D A T R I A N G L E
E R N E ■ E R O S E ■ C O D A
L O O N ■ R E N T S ■ E R S T
```

6

```
EARTH ANTI  CAR
AROOM LEAN  AREA
STARSEARCH  LARD
TENT  SMOKE  ASIA
      GPO  RASHER
ELATE STAIN
SABENA OUTDOES
THESUNALSORISES
 RETITLE RESTED
  NIFTY WEEPS
ARISEN  EDS
MIRE OPINE  BRAS
PLEA MOONSTRUCK
LENT  ISLE BELIE
EYE  CHAD  SWEDE
```

7

```
PATIENT  HAIRDO
ADAGIOS  ORDAINS
DEFENSEATTORNEY
SETTEE STU  EGAN
       COEUR ROLE
GOINTOLABOR
INTERNE   ABATE
MEANIES  ALTERED
PALEO     VEERING
      SHIPOFSTATE
BUST  IDONT
ANTI TIO  TAIWAN
SCALESOFJUSTICE
EARDRUM  ORIENTS
 STEEPS  ENTREES
```

8

```
ASHES AURA  ERMA
SPARE ERIC  NOON
POINTOFNORETURN
STREAM  OSAGES
     EARS SPIES
LAMB RECITAL
ASIA LENIN  LIT
WESTPOINTCADETS
SAT ARETE  INCA
   TRIDENT BOHR
 SLAVE DDAY
STALIN  RIFLES
COMESTOTHEPOINT
ORAN ABIE  ERATO
WEST LIEN  STROP
```

9

```
CAMP SWAB  QUACK
OLEO TILL  UNCLE
WORKINGVACATION
LEVER GAIL ADDS
      REAL SAWN
ASPS NEVERAGAIN
STU AIRY ALLUDE
CAPON SIC  SEDER
ARABIC NOAH RAF
PRETTYUGLY SASS
     RAGS LEFT
ESAU NUDE  ORATE
NONDAIRYCREAMER
DATED ENTO IMAN
SPIRE REST TOME
```

10

```
SINS HERD  MASTS
TMEN ERIE  EXTRA
RATE WILT  ALAIN
ARTLINKLETTER
FELLS  SHY  WIZ
ETE ROTATE CARE
    PALER SCARED
   FREDCOUPLES
STEALS ORION
AIRY TAMEST CAM
LEO QED  HEAVE
  CHARLIEJOINER
IDIOT IDLE  GANG
MITLA BEAR  EDGE
PAYER SANK  RAES
```

11

H	A	V	E			U	S	E	S		S	A	G	A
I	M	A	G	E		P	O	G	O		A	M	O	S
S	I	N	G	L	E	S	B	A	R		T	E	R	N
	R	E	S	A	L	E		D	E	R	A	N	G	E
		L	I	T				E	N	D	E	R		
U	R	S	A		E	S	C	A	R	P				
N	I	O	B	E			A	R	O	U	S	E	S	
D	O	U	B	L	E	O	R	N	O	T	H	I	N	G
	T	R	E	M	B	L	E		E	E	R	I	E	
		O	B	E	Y	E	D		D	E	P	T		
A	A	R	O	N			L	O	A					
G	R	U	N	T	E	D		A	L	L	O	U	T	
L	U	M	S		T	R	I	P	L	E	P	L	A	Y
O	B	O	E		N	O	D	S		C	A	N	O	E
W	A	R	T		A	P	S	E		L	A	S	T	

12

♥	I	E	R		G	R	A	B		W	A	R	M	♥
S	T	A	Y		R	E	A	R		A	R	E	A	L
H	E	R	E		E	C	R	U		S	T	A	R	E
A	R	A		S	T	E		C	A	P		L	T	S
P	A	C		T	A	N	D	E	M	S		T	I	S
E	T	H	E	R		T	I	L	E		F	O	A	L
D	E	E	M	E	D		S	E	N		O	R	L	Y
			O	P	E	N	♥	E	D	L	Y			
B	R	A	T		T	O	E		S	I	E	G	E	S
R	A	R	E		E	T	N	A		A	R	E	N	A
O	V	A		D	R	E	S	S	E	R		N	S	C
K	E	N		E	S	P		P	A	S		O	U	R
E	L	T	O	N		A	P	E	S		S	E	R	E
N	E	X	U	S		D	I	C	E		U	S	E	D
♥	R	A	T	E		S	E	T	S		R	E	D	♥

13

C	H	U	M		A	S	S	E	T		A	S	S	T
I	O	N	A		G	E	E	S	E		B	A	T	H
A	R	M	S		E	L	A	T	E		A	L	E	E
	S	E	C	O	N	D	M	A	N	A	S	S	A	S
S	E	R		A	D	O		S	H	A	K	E		
C	H	I	C	K	A	M	A	U	G	A				
R	I	T	A	S		T	R	A	P		M	V	I	
E	D	E	N		A	M	E	N	D		G	E	O	L
W	E	D		A	C	E	S		S	E	L	L	S	
		C	H	A	T	T	A	N	O	O	G	A		
A	C	T	O	R		A	S	U		D	O	S		
F	R	E	D	E	R	I	C	K	S	B	U	R	G	
T	I	R	E		A	G	R	E	E		P	A	R	D
O	M	I	T		P	O	E	M	S		O	M	A	N
N	E	S	S		T	R	E	E	S		N	A	D	A

14

L	I	S	P		P	A	T	S		A	B	C	S
O	D	O	R	S		A	L	O	T		S	L	U	E
B	L	U	E	C	O	L	L	A	R		T	U	R	N
	E	L	M	E	R		D	E	A	R	E	S	T	
		I	N	I	T			S	N	I	P	E		
F	I	B	S	T	E	R		A	S	I	D	E		
O	G	L	E		N	I	P	S		L	E	N	D	S
L	O	U		T	O	R	S	O			C	O	E	
D	R	E	G	S		D	O	E	R		S	I	R	E
	B	R	I	B	E		T	A	M	A	L	E	S	
	B	O	O	Z	E		S	T	A	N				
S	I	N	C	E	R	E		O	R	D	E	R		
A	N	N	E		B	L	U	E	R	I	B	B	O	N
D	E	E	R		E	L	S	E		A	A	R	O	N
A	T	T	Y		R	E	E	L		R	O	M	E	

15

A	W	E	D		I	N	C	U	R		G	L	E	N
C	A	L	I		G	O	O	S	E		L	E	V	I
T	H	E	S	O	U	N	D	O	F	M	U	S	I	C
	L	E	A	D	A				A	I	S	L	E	
	B	I	N	D		A	M	I	N					
B	E	L	L	S	A	R	E	R	I	N	G	I	N	G
A	D	I	E	T		E	A	R	L		M	I	R	
S	I	N	S		D	A	T	E	D		R	E	N	I
I	C	E		I	M	U	S		S	E	T	O	N	
S	T	R	I	K	E	U	P	T	H	E	B	A	N	D
	L	I	S	P		S	O	R	E					
B	R	A	I	N			O	I	L	E	D			
L	A	C	A	G	E	A	U	X	F	O	L	L	E	S
O	V	I	D		G	E	N	I	I		E	M	M	Y
W	E	D	S		G	R	I	S	T		D	O	I	N

16

```
ACTI   BLED  THROW
LORN   ROAD  HOOCH
FOOTLOOSE   WROTE
ALPHONSE    GASTON
     ETTE   TORE
GOP  TENFOOTPOLE
CRANE    AND  LUIS
LORE   MATES  ATNO
ENDS   AMS   SYRUP
FOOTINMOUTH   ESS
     LMNO   NEAT
TOBIAS   LEADOFFS
AMONG   PUSSYFOOT
LANGE  PACE   FARO
CRASS  DUOS   SLAP
```

17

```
AROMA   FLEW   APED
MESAS   IONA   LIME
PASTPERFORMANCE
SPAS   METS   AMEER
        SID   SHORE
BALLET   IOTA
ALIEN  INKER   EMS
ISNOTAGUARANTEE
LOT   IVORY   NORMA
       MORE  METEOR
SINEW         FOE
CANON   ALAD   LIEU
OFFUTURERESULTS
TEEN   SIAM   IRENE
ERRS   OARS   TEXAS
```

18

```
CRAFT    FANTAN
EAGLED   ALERTED
STEELE   STEALER
STIRS  PETER   ADE
HMO  HALTER   ANIS
EONS   COED   ANTES
WISEGUYS   ROTARY
       RATS   LONI
AERATE   BEDECKED
GRAPE  FATE   SNEE
HATE  WONTON   IRA
ASA  PARSE   ASTIN
SETTING   REBATE
TRAINEE   SPODES
  STEEDS   ABORT
```

19

```
ALUM   PENS   BAGEL
MENU   OVAL   IVORY
ANDS   TATA   LOLLS
DOESADOGSLIFE
        ATE   LOD
PRESTO  WHEW   BAT
RENTA  FOOD   MULE
OFTENTIMESBEGIN
VERT   IDES   ALLEE
ORE   UPON   ABSENT
       OSU   UNE
WITHPUPPYLOVE
DANTE   ROTO   PELT
ALGER   GOON   ERMA
BEERS   ERNE   NOON
```

20

```
LAPSE   MCS    SATE
ELIHU   ARP   MERRY
SELIG   GUARANTEE
 GENERIC   IRISES
     GNU   IMAGO
STALER   VOTARIES
TOLET  CEDAR   CAN
ENORM   ORE   ELATE
ATO   ARABS   TIMER
MONALISA   OFFEND
     YENTL   NAE
ASSESS   INERTIA
SPEAKEASY   RIDGE
TANYA   DTS   AMEER
ANTE   ESE   READS
```

21

	C	O	R	K	S			R	A	V	A	G	E
	R	A	V	I	N	E		R	E	L	I	V	E	S
B	E	N	E	F	I	T		E	X	I	G	E	N	T
A	M	A	R	E	T	T	O	S		T	O	R	T	E
L	A	S	T			E	M	I	L		R	A	L	E
L	I	T	U	P		R	A	D	A	R		G	E	M
S	N	A	R	E	S		N	E	G	A	T	E	S	
		E	A	T	S		D	O	P	E	
	L	E	S	S	E	N	S		S	I	L	I	C	A
M	E	X		E	P	I	C	S		D	E	M	O	N
A	G	E	D		S	P	A	T		S	P	A	N	
R	U	M	O	R		P	R	O	S	E	C	U	T	E
I	M	P	L	O	D	E		D	E	V	O	T	E	E
N	E	T	C	O	R	D		G	R	I	P	E	D	
A	S	S	E	T	S			E	E	L	E	D	

22

B	A	L	D		H	A	R	T	E		C	O	S	T
I	L	A	Y		O	N	E	R	S		L	U	K	E
D	O	W	N	A	N	D	O	U	T		O	T	I	S
S	E	N	A	T	O	R	S		A	L	S	O	P	S
			M	I	R	E		S	T	E	E	N	
O	T	O	O	L	E		C	H	E	E	T	A	H	S
L	O	U		T	E	R	R	A		S	E	L	A	H
M	O	T	S		S	E	E	M	S		D	I	N	O
A	N	T	I	C		L	E	E	K	S		M	O	O
N	E	O	N	A	T	E	S		I	N	A	B	I	T
			L	I	G	H	T		S	L	I	D	
A	B	U	S	E	R		S	H	I	P	M	A	T	E
W	A	N	T		O	U	T	O	F	S	I	G	H	T
O	N	C	E		B	L	U	E	T		T	R	E	E
L	E	H	R		S	E	N	D	S		S	A	Y	S

23

S	H	E	D	S		B	O	G	Y		O	P	E	N
P	I	X	I	E		E	G	O	S		P	I	L	E
A	V	A	N	T	G	A	R	D	E		T	E	L	E
R	E	M		T	R	U	E		R	A	I	D	E	D
		E	L	I	X	I	R		M	O	A	N	S	
F	A	B	L	E	D		S	E	C	A	N	T	
O	B	I	S			A	H	W	A	Z		E	R	A
A	B	L	A	T	E	S		E	Y	E	B	R	O	W
M	E	L		R	A	T	E	D			A	R	A	L
	E	D	I	T	E	D		S	A	Y	E	R	S	
A	N	T	I	C		R	U	M	P	U	S	
D	O	D	G	E	S		C	O	A	T		D	A	B
O	B	O	E		P	L	A	T	D	U	J	O	U	R
P	L	U	S		O	A	T	H		M	A	L	T	A
T	E	X	T		T	Y	E	S		N	Y	L	O	N

24

D	O	M	E	S		M	A	S	K			U	M	P
A	L	I	V	E		A	L	I	E		A	P	E	R
Y	I	N	A	N	D	Y	A	N	G		G	A	L	A
S	O	T		A	D	O	R	E	S		A	N	E	W
				T	E	R	M		W	I	D	E	N	
L	A	D	L	E		S	E	S	T	I	N	A	
A	L	O	E			D	E	E	R		B	U	N	
D	A	W	D	L	E	R		A	N	E	M	O	N	E
S	I	N		O	M	A	R			A	U	T	O	
		A	D	A	P	T	E	D		G	E	T	O	N
P	I	N	E	D		N	U	D	E		
R	O	D	E		S	T	E	R	E	O		C	P	A
A	T	O	M		N	O	W	A	N	D	T	H	E	N
T	A	U	S		I	R	A	N		E	V	I	C	T
E	S	T			P	E	L	T		S	A	C	K	S

25

R	E	B	E	L		E	G	B	D	F		W	A	G
A	R	O	M	A		B	R	O	A	D		E	E	L
M	A	X	I	M		B	O	X	C	A	M	E	R	A
		O	T	I	S		V	E	E		O	D	I	N
A	L	F		A	C	H	E	D		R	A	Y	E	D
D	U	F	F		H	E	L	I	C	E	S	
M	A	I	L	B	O	X		N	A	B		S	H	E
E	N	C	O	I	L			J	O	S	H	U	A	
N	N	E		T	A	J		B	O	X	C	A	R	S
			P	E	R	U	S	A	L		I	D	L	E
O	P	A	L	S		K	H	M	E	R		O	Y	L
R	I	C	E		O	E	R		S	H	A	W	
S	Q	U	A	W	K	B	O	X		E	M	B	E	R
O	U	T		I	L	O	V	E		A	B	O	V	E
N	E	E		T	A	X	E	S		S	I	X	E	D

26

```
A C A T   C A T E R   A S S
R A G E S   O R A T E   M I T
C R U N C H B E R R Y   O N E
O P E N A I R   P E N A N C E
      L E A     A N G E L
H A R P E R S F E R R Y
A L I A S   I R E D   P O M
R E N D   P A L E D   J A V A
P E G   T I N T   S O R E R
    M A T T H E W P E R R Y
I B E A M     C H E
N I A G A R A   H E N R E I D
L O S   L O N D O N D E R R Y
A T E   E S T E E   S A G A N
W A D   S E E M S   L O N E
```

27

```
H A L L   A L M S   S I L O
A R I A S   C O A L   K N A P
J A M U P J E L L Y T I G H T
I B E R I A   L I L I   E R S
      E R M A   G Y P
J E L L Y B E A N   T E V Y E
A N A   S O B   O C E A N
M O T I F   N O N   P O R T O
E L E N I   V I P   D E C
S A X O N   J E L L Y F I S H
      E M U   S A U L
A D E   L A R K   S K O A L S
J E L L Y R O L L M O R T O N
A L I T   T R E E   N A O M I
R E E D   A S E A   S P A T
```

28

```
T A P   A S S U M E   D R A B
A V A   S H U T I N   E A V E
R E P   P A P E R H A N G E R
P R E S I D E S   A T T E S T
    R A R E R   A N T I
E U C L I D   B I C U S P I D
A S H E N   H I D E   T A R O
R E A   S H Y N E S S   P E N
L U S T   O D D S   O B E S E
S P E A K E R S   E C A R T E
    R E D O   M U R A T
A D A G I O   L O C A L I Z E
P A P E R W E I G H T   G E L
E R S T   N A T U R E   E R A
S E E S   S T E L E S   R O N
```

29

```
S C A T   L A R D   T H I S
R A S H   A L O E   R O O S T
S T I R   W E A R   E C O L E
O N E E Y E D M O N S T E R
      S T E   D E I S T
O N E H O R S E T O W N
P A T E N   L E E R S   R O W
A P A R   A L T   L A M A
L E S   A B N E R   S A V E R
    O N E T R A C K M I N D
  K O R D A   H I E
O N E A R M E D B A N D I T
G E S T E   G O O F   U V E A
R E T O W   A D Z E   C A R R
E D E R   D O O R   K N I T
```

30

```
F L E X   S W A P   M A A M
R O R Y   A C A S E   A L D O
E L I Z A B E T H T A Y L O R
T A N   L I N T Y   R E I G N
    C E D E   S I R
A P L A C E I N T H E S U N
T R I P   U R A L   N O V
T Y N E   O P R A H   S I N E
N O D   A C E S   H O E R
  R A I N T R E E C O U N T Y
    B I O   A H O T
O B J E T   M A R I N   I L L
C O U R A G E O F L A S S I E
H A D I   A N N U L   A L F A
S T O A   D U E L   W E E K
```

31

```
W O V E N ■ M A P L E ■ W A D
I N A N E ■ A L L A Y ■ A V A
G O L D E N G L O B E ■ Y O M
■ ■ D E U S ■ L E N I N
M O D U L E S ■ F E E L E R S
E R A S E D ■ T O R S O S ■
A B I E S ■ R E A M S ■ W A S
N I L S ■ F I R M A ■ B O N A
S T Y ■ B O O R S ■ P O R G Y
■ P E L O T A ■ B I L L I E
B A L L O T S ■ B R O O D E R
A L A M O ■ S E E N ■ ■
K I N ■ M O T H E R E A R T H
E V E ■ E L I O T ■ E L I A S
S E T ■ R E N T S ■ R E A C T
```

32

```
G L U M ■ A T L A S ■ E L A L
L I S A ■ R H E T T ■ R I T A
A M E R I C A S F R E E D O M
D E D I C A T E ■ I N C O M E
■ N E D S ■ S C O T ■ ■
P A L A C E ■ S A K S ■ N A B
R I A T A ■ S E V E ■ D U M A
I N D E P E N D E N C E D A Y
A G E S ■ T E E S ■ O P I N E
M E N ■ C H A R ■ S P R E A D
■ S H E D ■ P A T E ■
E S T H E R ■ P A L I S A D E
P Y R O T E C H N I C S H O W
O N E R ■ A R D E N ■ O O Z E
S E E N ■ L I S L E ■ R Y E S
```

33

```
H U M A N ■ B A T H ■ A B A B
A B O L T ■ A R E A ■ S A G E
H E R S H E Y B A R ■ T R U E
A R N O ■ G O O S E ■ A B E T
■ F O U R ■ T R E S S
R A B B I S ■ S P A R E R ■
A W A R D ■ U N I ■ S S S
P A R A D E S ■ N Y M P H E T
S Y M ■ L A C ■ M A O R I
■ I B E R I A ■ P E P P E R
L A T E R ■ R O A D ■
L I Z A ■ S H I N S ■ D O R A
A D V T ■ P A S S T H E B A R
M E A T ■ A L E E ■ A L I K E
A S H Y ■ R E N T ■ M I T E S
```

34

```
R A Y E ■ D U P E ■ P L U G S
E L E V ■ O R A L ■ R O M E O
S T L O ■ W A L L T O W A L L
P E L L M E L L ■ I T E ■
■ O V A L S ■ S N O R I N G
T O W E R S ■ D E S C ■ L E R
H U B S ■ C A M E O ■ L E E
U T E ■ I L L W I L L ■ O S E
M E L ■ M O O N S ■ A G O N
B A L ■ M V P S ■ R A C I N E
S T Y M I E S ■ L I L A C ■
■ E N L ■ R O L L C A L L
V O L L E Y B A L L ■ I L I A
A R I O N ■ A B L E ■ A L O T
T R E N T ■ N E S T ■ S Y N E
```

35

```
A L A S ■ B A N D S ■ G L O B
R O M P ■ O W N E R ■ L O N I
A L A I ■ L E E I A C O C C A
B A S K E T S ■ V A R I E S
■ E T S ■ C O S I ■
B E L L E ■ S P A ■ T A S S O
E R I E ■ H E A R S E ■ A P R
R O B E R T E D W A R D L E E
E S E ■ A S T R A Y ■ O S L O
T E L L S ■ H E X ■ O R A L S
■ E P E E ■ F B I ■
C H A F E D ■ A R I S I N G
L E E T R E V I N O ■ L O A N
A R O O ■ N I K O N ■ E T N A
P E N N ■ S P E N T ■ E A S T
```

36

REWED · HUP · TACTS
ABODE · USA · ALOHA
WORDGAMES · XAXES
LADY · SIRS · IMAMS
STS · HAD · WACO ·
· QTIP · WONA · WAS
AGUAS · WORDBOOKS
LOAM · WORDS · BRIG
FOREWORDS · DIDNT
ADE · ANDY · PIES ·
· ACTS · COX · WPA
SLINK · AJAR · MOAN
LUNDI · LASTWORDS
ACARE · AVE · ENTRE
PETER · DAY · ETHEL

37

SAMBA · ACNE · SWAG
ARIEL · SHUN · OHIO
VANNAWHITE · NILE
ELIS · HENS · DATES
· RENE · METED ·
NEWTON · SEESAW ·
ETHEL · BEAST · ADA
STILLER · CAROTID
TAT · TRASH · UPEND
· ELOISE · SCARES
· SHAPE · ABET ·
SLOPS · AWOL · SLIT
PIUS · PEARLWHITE
ELSE · ERLE · ROLEX
DYED · GOLD · YEAST

38

MACE · EMBARK · VON
ALAN · MAIDEN · IRA
RIDDICKBOWE · OAR
IVE · DEES · REALLY
SETTLER · MILLI ·
· OED · LATEENS ·
FABER · FOYER · BIN
AMOS · IOTAS · BOZO
BED · ECRUS · BOWER
· SIGNETS · BLY ·
· DITCH · HEADSET
DODGER · YEAR · AXE
AXL · BEAUXGESTES
TEE · BARREL · HIRT
ANY · EMPIRE · ANTS

39

DORIS · ASST · FADS
EXIST · SLUR · EDIT
LEFTATHOME · ZERO
· NEONS · POPS · EGO
· DES · ALFRED
DETESTED · NIL ·
AMON · STES · COBRA
MIDDLEOFTHEROAD
PROSE · NERO · ARNE
· UTE · RINGLETS
POMPOM · PEA ·
ARE · NEMO · SLASH
SITS · RIGHTOFWAY
HEAP · GLEE · ORATE
ALLY · EDEN · TOMES

40

HALFEAGLE · AGAVE
OVERTURES · LACED
GETACROSS · ASTIN
GRIN · ASSET · PINA
SYNCH · OXYGEN ·
· SOLAN · PUDGE
ARM · COFFEETABLE
ROOM · MARLS · LUBE
POWERBROKER · GAR
· DECCA · METAL ·
· DHARMA · NAPPE
DADA · DOLCE · PERN
ASONE · ROUGHSPOT
LEWIS · TELEMETER
LANCE · ASTRODOME

41

C	O	S	T	A		C	A	S	E		V	I	T	A
A	P	L	U	S		A	I	N	T		E	N	O	S
R	E	I	N	S		T	M	A	N		R	C	M	P
P	R	E	G	N	A	N	T	P	A	U	S	E		
E	A	R	S		R	I	O			P	U	N	Y	
			T	E	R	P		M	I	S	S	T	E	P
I	S	M	E	N	E		G	O	B	I		I	M	A
S	T	A	N	D	A	N	D	D	E	L	I	V	E	R
L	O	N		O	R	E	S		R	O	D	E	N	T
A	M	H	E	R	S	T		P	I	N	E			
	P	A	T	S		P	E	A		N	O	D	S	
		T	H	E	P	A	R	E	N	T	T	R	A	P
J	E	T	E		E	R	I	K		R	I	A	T	A
O	V	A	L		G	A	Z	E		A	F	T	E	R
Y	E	N	S		S	L	E	D		M	Y	E	R	S

42

WARPS RACE CELL
IMETA ELLA ARLO
REDASABEET BIAS
ENOS SAGAS ACNE
SATAN ONTO
COROT ERS LAH
ARENAS ELI EEL
SEDATES REVERSE
ASH IAM TERETE
EGO END RADAR
BRAN LOUTS
WARM ATOMS ARKS
ERIE REDBUTTONS
RENT ERLE AMBIT
EDGE AYER POETS

43

WHELP REPS SASS
PIKER OXEN ALOU
ACEVENTURA VANS
ICIER GLORIA
PICNIC BOGEYMAN
ADA SET TYR
LINA SASH OPALS
LOOKATTHEBIRDIE
STEAL TYRO EDEN
IDO SOP UGO
PARAVION DRAPER
OLIVER ISLES
PAGE EAGLESCOUT
EMIR CLEO TAUPE
SODS TART OPTIC

44

APSIS NAZI SLAW
GRANT OMAN PINA
TENCOMMANDMENTS
SPEAKEASY ALDEN
ENDS ATLAST
ABOARD ORTS
SOON EERIE SST
HUNDREDYEARSWAR
ETA ORIEL AUTO
SCAT ZOOMED
CAMPOS STUN
OLEIC SCHLEMIEL
CASTOFTHOUSANDS
ACHE RAMS EIGHT
SKYS OBOE CLASS

45

EDEN TREE TIMER
DONE HARM INURE
GNAW EMIT RUSTY
ANCHOVIES ASHES
RETAKES ODER
VAT DALE ORE
HOMEY CORDS OIL
AMEN WHOME HMOS
DOA CHARY FOSSE
JOT HUTS LAM
BEEP SAVEDUP
WHALE PEPPERONI
HALLS IZOD UNTO
ALLIE EROO NEIN
MOSES RANG SEES

46

H	E	L	P	S	■	B	L	O	C	■	A	D	I	N
A	D	I	E	U	■	A	I	D	A	■	N	A	B	E
S	T	E	P	B	Y	S	T	E	P	■	E	Y	E	S
■	■	■	P	A	S	■	■	T	H	W	A	R	T	■
M	O	O	L	A	H	■	D	D	A	Y	■	F	I	E
A	L	V	A	R	O	■	I	R	I	S	■	T	A	D
P	E	E	P	■	O	N	E	O	N	O	N	E	■	■
S	O	R	E	S	■	I	T	O	■	N	O	R	T	E
■	A	L	L	I	N	A	L	L	■	M	D	I	V	■
M	I	N	■	O	M	E	R	■	I	D	E	A	T	E
I	N	D	■	S	P	R	Y	■	C	A	N	Y	O	N
C	L	O	T	H	O	■	N	I	K	■	■	■	■	■
R	O	V	E	■	S	I	D	E	T	O	S	I	D	E
O	V	E	N	■	E	L	I	A	■	T	O	W	E	L
N	E	R	D	■	D	E	E	R	■	A	T	O	L	L

47

B	A	S	R	A	■	C	L	O	G	■	T	E	R	I
O	N	T	O	P	■	H	O	W	E	■	E	L	A	N
D	O	U	B	L	E	O	R	N	O	T	H	I	N	G
E	N	D	■	O	T	O	E	■	M	I	R	A	G	E
■	■	A	M	A	S	■	S	E	R	A	■	■	■	■
D	O	U	B	L	E	E	N	T	E	N	T	E	■	■
B	O	R	N	■	■	A	I	R	S	■	I	A	M	■
A	L	O	T	■	P	A	R	T	Y	■	O	G	R	E
T	E	N	■	B	E	L	T	■	■	B	E	N	T	■
■	D	O	U	B	L	E	H	E	A	D	E	R	S	■
■	■	S	A	L	E	■	X	R	A	Y	■	■	■	■
E	M	B	A	L	M	■	K	O	N	G	■	D	A	B
D	O	U	B	L	E	I	N	D	E	M	N	I	T	Y
I	T	L	L	■	L	I	E	U	■	A	R	N	I	E
T	E	L	E	■	L	I	E	S	■	R	A	S	P	S

48

E	L	I	Z	A	■	B	E	L	■	B	O	M	B	■
M	Y	G	A	L	■	A	C	E	■	L	U	N	A	R
M	O	O	N	L	I	G	H	T	S	O	N	A	T	A
A	N	T	E	■	R	E	O	■	A	U	D	I	T	S
■	■	A	I	L	■	A	M	P	E	R	E	S	■	■
A	C	R	O	S	S	■	R	I	S	E	■	■	■	■
T	A	I	N	T	■	G	O	S	H	■	A	C	H	E
O	N	C	E	I	N	A	B	L	U	E	M	O	O	N
P	E	E	R	■	E	L	I	E	■	L	O	V	E	D
■	■	S	T	A	N	■	A	S	S	E	S	S	■	■
M	O	S	L	E	M	S	■	O	R	E	■	■	■	■
O	C	T	A	N	E	■	E	T	C	■	I	N	C	A
T	H	E	M	A	N	I	N	T	H	E	M	O	O	N
T	E	N	E	T	■	D	O	E	■	G	A	M	I	N
E	R	O	S	■	I	S	R	■	O	M	E	N	S	■

49

P	E	W	■	E	D	G	E	■	A	D	O	P	T	■
E	L	I	E	■	C	R	A	G	■	B	O	G	I	E
A	S	S	N	■	H	O	B	G	O	B	L	I	N	S
K	E	P	T	■	O	P	S	■	R	E	E	V	E	S
■	■	R	T	E	S	■	G	A	S	S	E	R	■	■
■	H	E	A	R	D	■	H	E	N	S	■	■	■	■
M	A	R	N	E	■	F	A	N	G	■	S	H	O	E
T	R	I	C	K	O	R	T	R	E	A	T	E	R	S
S	P	E	E	■	R	I	C	E	■	B	E	R	E	T
■	■	C	A	S	H	■	S	L	E	D	S	■	■	■
■	A	E	R	A	T	E	■	A	P	E	R	■	■	■
A	P	P	O	S	E	■	F	I	R	■	A	D	A	M
G	H	O	S	T	S	T	O	R	Y	■	G	A	P	E
R	I	D	E	R	■	O	R	E	L	■	E	R	S	E
A	D	E	N	O	■	E	D	D	Y	■	N	E	T	■

50

■	■	■	S	T	R	E	P	■	P	A	C	E	S	■
A	B	C	■	I	R	E	N	E	■	E	P	H	O	R
S	L	O	W	B	O	A	T	T	O	C	H	I	N	A
T	O	M	E	■	O	R	E	■	R	A	I	N	■	■
A	C	M	E	■	P	E	R	■	I	N	D	E	N	T
■	■	U	P	I	■	R	E	E	F	■	S	A	O	■
C	A	N	Y	O	N	■	D	A	I	S	■	E	I	N
A	L	I	■	W	A	D	■	R	C	A	■	P	A	T
S	O	S	■	A	T	O	M	■	E	S	C	U	D	O
E	N	T	■	U	S	E	R	■	K	H	Z	■	■	■
S	E	C	T	O	R	■	D	I	G	■	E	Z	R	A
■	■	H	O	P	E	■	I	C	E	■	C	L	A	P
C	H	I	N	E	S	E	C	H	E	C	K	E	R	S
L	I	N	E	N	■	S	A	L	S	A	■	S	E	E
U	M	A	S	S	■	S	L	Y	E	R	■	■	■	■

51

A	L	I	B	I		I	D	E	A		R	A	G	S
B	E	T	O	N		K	I	L	N		A	G	R	A
E	A	S	Y	D	O	E	S	I	T		T	E	A	L
T	R	A	D	E	D		H	A	H		I	N	C	A
		X	E	S			E	M	O	T	E	D		
A	M	M	O		R	E	R	O	S	E				
S	E	A	R	S		D	A	N	I	O		I	O	N
H	A	S	T	E	M	A	K	E	S	W	A	S	T	E
E	L	K		R	A	T	E	D		S	P	L	I	T
		F	L	E	D	G	E		T	E	S	S		
C	A	R	U	S	O		E	D	S					
E	R	I	N		D	U	D		I	N	U	R	E	D
L	E	A	D		O	N	E	A	T	A	T	I	M	E
L	A	T	E		R	I	M	S		G	A	M	M	A
O	S	A	R		S	T	O	P		S	H	E	A	F

52

C	A	P	E		L	U	C	I	D		A	S	P	S
A	P	E	S		A	T	A	R	I		S	K	E	W
M	A	K	E	T	R	A	C	K	S		S	E	R	A
P	R	O		O	S	H	A		P	A	I	D	U	P
S	T	E	P	P	E		O	D	E	S	S	A		
		R	O	N	S		I	N	S	I	D	E	R	
A	C	T	O	F		T	O	T	S			D	L	I
H	E	A	D	F	O	R	T	H	E	H	I	L	L	S
A	R	K		V	O	T	E		A	P	E	A	K	
S	T	E	E	P	E	D		R	E	D	S			
	A	D	O	R	E	S		I	D	E	A	L	S	
A	P	H	I	D	S		A	S	T	I		L	E	I
S	L	I	T		H	I	T	T	H	E	R	O	A	D
K	O	K	O		O	R	A	L	E		A	N	N	E
S	T	E	R		T	E	N	O	R		T	E	S	S

53

	A	R	K	S		C	O	O	E	R		A	L	P
	L	E	I	A		H	A	U	T	E		R	Y	E
	A	L	L	T	H	E	K	I	N	G	S	M	E	N
P	R	I	N	C	E	S	S	D	A	I	S	Y		
E	I	S		H	E	S		A	S	S	T			
E	C	H	O					S	O	L	E			
	R	E	S	T	O	R	E	D		W	E	D		
T	H	E	E	M	P	E	R	O	R	J	O	N	E	S
V	A	T		S	A	L	T	I	E	S	T			
S	W	A	B				T	A	C	K				
	I	D	I	O		L	O	A		R	H	O		
	P	R	I	N	C	E	O	F	T	I	D	E	S	
L	O	R	D	O	F	T	H	E	F	L	I	E	S	
A	X	E		D	E	A	R	S		A	I	N	T	
X	Y	Z		E	R	L	E	S		S	I	T	S	

54

S	L	E	E	T		A	N	T	E		T	S	A	R
R	A	T	I	O		S	A	R	A		R	U	L	E
S	O	U	R	G	R	A	P	E	S		A	G	O	G
	S	I	E	G	E		A	S	I	A		A	H	A
		L	A	S		S	E	V	E	R	A	L		
I	N	S	P	E	C	T	S		R	I	N	D		
R	O	W	E		H	I	P	S		S	T	A	L	L
A	T	E	S	T		L	I	P		O	R	D	I	E
S	E	E	T	O		T	E	E	S		E	D	N	A
	T	O	U	R		D	E	W	Y	E	Y	E	D	
M	O	B	S	T	E	R		D	O	E				
A	I	R		S	U	E	S		R	A	I	L	S	
P	L	I	E		B	I	T	T	E	R	R	O	O	T
L	E	A	N		E	N	O	S		N	O	R	M	A
E	R	R	S		N	E	A	P		S	N	E	E	R

55

W	E	P	T		I	D	E	S		P	R	I	M	O
A	L	O	E		N	E	A	P		R	E	V	E	L
C	A	P	S		P	I	C	O		O	L	A	N	D
O	N	E	T	O	U	C	H	O	F	V	E	N	U	S
		A	N	T	E		N	O	O	N				
P	L	A	T	E	S		B	B	C		T	A	L	L
L	E	V	E	R		M	A	I	A		S	H	O	O
U	N	O		W	E	I	L	L			S	T	P	
M	Y	N	A		H	A	L	L		S	P	I	T	E
P	A	S	S		O	N	S		L	E	R	N	E	R
		P	L	O	D		I	A	G	O				
T	H	R	E	E	P	E	N	N	Y	O	P	E	R	A
Y	E	A	R	N		R	O	B	E		J	A	I	L
P	E	P	S	I		E	V	E	R		E	T	N	A
O	L	S	E	N		D	A	D	S		T	S	K	S

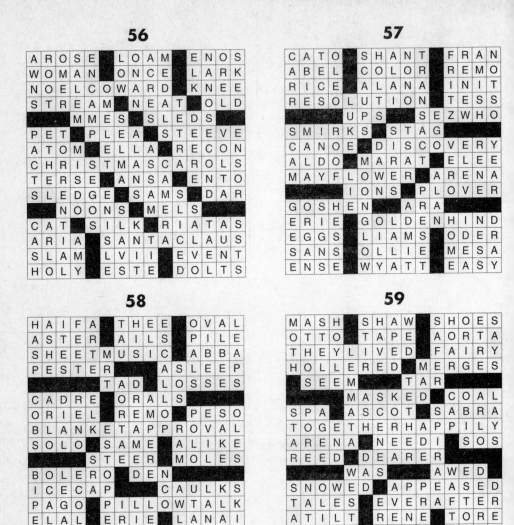

56

```
A R O S E   L O A M   E N O S
W O M A N   O N C E   L A R K
N O E L C O W A R D   K N E E
S T R E A M   N E A T   O L D
      M M E S   S L E D S
P E T   P L E A   S T E E V E
A T O M   E L L A   R E C O N
C H R I S T M A S C A R O L S
T E R S E   A N S A   E N T O
S L E D G E   S A M S   D A R
    N O O N S   M E L S
C A T   S I L K   R I A T A S
A R I A   S A N T A C L A U S
S L A M   L V I I   E V E N T
H O L Y   E S T E   D O L T S
```

57

```
C A T O   S H A N T   F R A N
A B E L   C O L O R   R E M O
R I C E   A L A N A   I N I T
R E S O L U T I O N   T E S S
      U P S   S E Z W H O
S M I R K S   S T A G
C A N O E   D I S C O V E R Y
A L D O   M A R A T   E L E E
M A Y F L O W E R   A R E N A
      I O N S   P L O V E R
G O S H E N   A R A
E R I E   G O L D E N H I N D
E G G S   L I A M S   O D E R
S A N S   O L L I E   M E S A
E N S E   W Y A T T   E A S Y
```

58

```
H A I F A   T H E E   O V A L
A S T E R   A I L S   P I L E
S H E E T M U S I C   A B B A
P E S T E R       A S L E E P
      T A D   L O S S E S
C A D R E   O R A L S
O R I E L   R E M O   P E S O
B L A N K E T A P P R O V A L
S O L O   S A M E   A L I K E
      S T E E R   M O L E S
B O L E R O   D E N
I C E C A P       C A U L K S
P A G O   P I L L O W T A L K
E L A L   E R I E   L A N A I
D A L E   L A D D   S H A N T
```

59

```
M A S H   S H A W   S H O E S
O T T O   T A P E   A O R T A
T H E Y L I V E D   F A I R Y
H O L L E R E D   M E R G E S
  S E E M   T A R
    M A S K E D   C O A L
S P A   A S C O T   S A B R A
T O G E T H E R H A P P I L Y
A R E N A   N E E D I   S O S
R E E D   D E A R E R
    W A S   A W E D
S N O W E D   A P P E A S E D
T A L E S   E V E R A F T E R
A T I L T   R E N E   T O R E
B O O T S   A R T Y   S P E D
```

60

```
I N C A   A R M E D   S N C C
N E R D   I H A V E   T O R A
O M A R   R E M I T   I T O R
N O B E L P E A C E P R I Z E
    A G O   T N T   C E E
C O M M E R C E   T A V E R N
C H A     T H E R E S A
C O R E   A R I   S C L C
    M A R T I N S   L E O
T A B U L A   E D U C T I V E
O R O   T I L   P O I
W E S H A L L O V E R C O M E
C O T Y   W A D E R   T A U T
A L O P   A M O N G   A T T Y
R E N E   Y A R D S   C H E M
```

61

```
. A C R E . M O D E L . E L F
E A R E D . A R O M A . V I E
G R E E N S T R E E T . E V E
G O T F A T . . S N E E R E D
S N E E . R O B . D R A G . .
. . R A I D E R S . G R A B .
P E G . O P E R A . D E E R E
S I R E N . S A D . E R E C T
I R E N E . S T I L E . N S A
S E E D . C A E S A R S . . .
. N A S A . S H Y . A R F S .
W A L T E R S . E A T E R Y .
I R A . W I N T E R G R E E N
T I N . O N I O N . H A S T E
H A D . N A P E S . A P E S .
```

62

```
C O P . . C A P O . H O P E S
O R A L . O N E A . O R O N O
M A K E S H O R T W O R K O F
E N I S L E . C H I T . E S T
R G S . A R N . . D E S . . .
. . T A K E A S H O R T C U T
B L A M E . V I E W . A L S O
L I N O . S A D A S . G O E R
A M I R . C H E R . J E S S E
H A S A S H O R T F U S E . .
. . . L A I . . Y I N . T A O
I V S . C Z A R . S T R I N G
G E T S H O R T C H A N G E D
O R A T E . G E R E . A H M E
R A B A T . O S I S . . T O N
```

63

```
M E M O . S M A C K . C R A B
A V I D . T A L O N . H O M E
J A N E M A R P L E . A L O E
O D D . E R I S . A R R E S T
R E S E R V E . E D E L . . .
. . L E E . L A S S I T E R .
J O E L . S C O T . T E R S E
U L C E R . H O E . S C E N E
M I C R O . A N N E . H E E L
P O L Y G A M Y . A M A . . .
. . Q U I P . G R E N A D E .
A R G U E R . A R T S . R E D
C A L E . M I K E H A M M E R
T R U E . A R I E L . G O R E
S E E N . N A N N Y . M R E D
```

64

```
R E G O . F A L L . . C O A T
E T O N . A D U E . R A M B O
S H O E . D O N T G I V E U P
T E D . B E L A . A G E N T S
S L A V E . P T E R O . . . .
. . D O L P H I N . R U F U S
R E V I L E . C O D . S O R A
E L I D E R S . S E C U R E S
N I C E . T A B . M O R A Y S
D E E D S . R E G I M E N . .
. . . K O A L A . E R A T O .
A F F A I R . L L B S . C A M
Y O U R D A Y J O B . I T S A
E R N E S . E A R L . R O T H
S E T S . . T R E S . A R E A
```

65

```
T U B A . G O F A R . U T A H
A R I D . A Z U R E . R O B E
P A L M . M O R N I N G D E W
A L L I . E N S . G U E S T S
. . E R A S E . A N I N . . .
I N T A C T . S T I T C H E D
S I D L E . S E A T . Y O R E
L O O . S A M P L E S . W V A
A B U T . N A T E . L E D I N
M E X I C A L I . S A X O N S
. . P O L L . P A P P Y . . .
U N E S C O . E O N . O O P S
P O S T A G E D U E . S U E T
D O M E . U N I T S . E D G E
O N E R . E G E S T . D O O M
```

66

```
B I T E S ■ B R O W ■ ■ R A P S
A R I E L ■ L A N E ■ E D A M
J O L L Y R O G E R ■ C U R E
A N T S ■ O B E S E ■ E L S A
■ ■ L O S ■ ■ W A S T E R
J E T S A M ■ S T O P S ■ ■
U N I O N ■ S H I L L ■ S P A
J O L L Y G O O D F E L L O W
U S E ■ A L O N E ■ N O I S E
■ ■ P R A T E ■ S T A T E D
S T E E D S ■ ■ T O Y ■ ■
A B M S ■ S N A I L ■ A C T S
L O O T ■ F E L L O W S H I P
A N T E ■ U R A L ■ A T O N E
D E E R ■ L O S S ■ G A P E D
```

67

```
O S A K A ■ S O A K ■ S T A Y
T R I A D ■ T A T A ■ C A V E
T A R Z A N O F T H E A P E S
■ ■ O M A R ■ O N E R ■ ■
O H I O ■ S E A R ■ R E E V E
R A N ■ H Y M N S ■ C Z A R
G U S T O ■ N E O P R E N E
■ L O R D G R E Y S T O K E ■
M A L A D I E S ■ S W I S H
A G E D ■ S C I O N ■ E S E
R E S E T ■ R A B E ■ C L A Y
■ ■ M O U E ■ E M M A ■ ■
M E T A R Z A N Y O U J A N E
A V E R ■ I N R E ■ L U N A R
P E E K ■ S T A R ■ E N T E R
```

68

```
W O L F E ■ A B E T ■ O C A T
I L E A C ■ R I P E ■ N O G O
P E A C H Y K E E N ■ A N E W
E S P I E S ■ N E E R ■ T E N
■ ■ E L E C ■ M E S A ■ ■
H A S ■ O R A N G E S T I C K
E T H A N ■ L O O N ■ E N O L
D R E I ■ P I V O T ■ N E N E
D I E S ■ A C E D ■ C O R G I
A P P L E P O L I S H ■ S A N
■ ■ S E V E ■ E T A L ■ ■
M A H ■ A R N E ■ E R O D E S
E R E I ■ B A N A N A S E A T
S T A R ■ O D O R ■ D E N S E
H Y D E ■ Y A W N ■ E S T E S
```

69

```
D I T T O ■ M A M A ■ A C T S
I D E A L ■ A B E L ■ T A R O
M O N K E Y S U I T ■ E T O N
E L S E ■ A S T R A L ■ B U G
■ ■ S P R A T ■ R E B U T S
J A R ■ U R G E ■ S E E R ■
I M A ■ C O E D ■ ■ A G R A
H E B R E W S ■ B A C K L O G
A B B A ■ S A R A ■ A P E
D A I S Y S ■ C L I P ■ R E D
■ T H A T ■ R A S P S ■ ■
P O E ■ M O M E N T ■ U S T A
A L A N ■ C O W C A T C H E R
T I R E ■ K N E E ■ A R E N T
H O S T ■ Y A R D ■ R E A D S
```

70

```
T A L C ■ O W E N S ■ A D A M
A R I A ■ P O S I T ■ I R M A
K I S S M E K A T E ■ S E E D
E S T H E R ■ E N G L A N D
■ ■ I R A T E ■ O R E M ■ ■
E T H E L ■ E S P ■ E D G A R
B R E R ■ D E S I R E ■ I T A
B I L ■ C A M E L O T ■ R B I
E E L ■ O P E N L Y ■ P L A N
D R O L L ■ R C A ■ M I S T Y
■ ■ D E E R ■ E R R O R ■ ■
C R O S S E R ■ U T O P I A
Y E L L ■ P A J A M A G A M E
D E L I ■ E R A T O ■ U L A R
S L Y E ■ L A M A R ■ E L M O
```

71

```
BOTH . OFTHE . HEN
ALOOF . TAHOE . APE
LEAVEITTOBEAVER
MODERN . HUB . NEED
. RANGE . ION .
SAD . LIAR . TREATS
ATE . NIK . TABOO
GILLIGANSISLAND
ALTAR . OWN . TEA
STARES . WAGS . ESS
. IDI . STEPS .
SOFA . EBB . SOLACE
THETHREESTOOGES
AIL . ERASE . FERNS
GOT . MATTE . SATE
```

72

```
NASTY . SLED . GRIT
ESTEE . PARE . ROTO
WHENTHECATSAWAY
SEWS . ONE . REPELS
. OLD . FINERY .
BECAME . PITT .
ACORN . BAJA . ACRE
THEMICEWILLPLAY
SODS . HENS . OSAGE
. SITS . BREWED
. SLOPES . ROD .
SHARIF . COY . OPAL
CATANDMOUSEGAME
ALIT . OMIT . ELGIN
BENE . MINE . LEEDS
```

73

```
LACES . SAGE . HATS
ADULT . OVUM . ALAI
CELLO . WISP . NELL
. STACKEDTHEDECK
. KIT . ALE .
CALLEDONESBLUFF
OREAD . OKIE . SOL
WRAP . SPIES . SURE
LOS . ELIS . SERGE
SWEETENEDTHEPOT
. ANE . EAU .
KEPTAPOKERFACE
EDIE . SIAM . FLOAT
PEER . ISLE . LARVA
INDY . NEED . ENDED
```

74

```
APPLE . STAG . DATA
CLEAR . LIMA . ERAS
HANGGLIDER . BOSS
ENDS . AMEND . ASTA
. SPY . ESTEEM
ETHICS . LANCE .
RHODA . SUSIE . TCU
LETITALLHANGOUT
EMS . TRULY . EAGLE
. BEAMS . TRYSTS
ASHARP . BUY .
LOOT . ALIEN . CAKE
BLAB . HANGAROUND
EERO . ONCE . AARON
EDDY . SKAT . PLATA
```

75

```
ALIMB . ADAMS . BAA
MARIO . MANIA . ARM
EVERYSPRING . ICI
RESALE . ETE . BRAD
. BEET . ASCENDS
ALEE . PEG . ASSET
TOGA . AERIAL .
AYOUNGMANSFANCY
. YESSES . PIPE
SPREE . SPA . PLAN
HAUNTED . TUNA .
ARID . XIS . LILIES
DAN . TURNSTOLOVE
ODE . EDGAR . BENET
WED . DEEPS . EDENS
```